Preface

The Junkers Ju 87 'Stuka' (a contraction of the German word *Sturzkampfflugzeug*, that is, dive bomber) was arguably the Luftwaffe's most recognisable aeroplane, with its inverted gull wings and fixed spatted undercarriage. Designed by Hermann Pohlmann as a dedicated dive bomber, the prototype first flew in 1935 and made its combat debut in 1937 with the Luftwaffe's Condor Legion during the Spanish Civil War. As history records, it then went on to serve Luftwaffe and Axis forces from the invasion of Poland in 1939 until the end of World War II, seeing combat in the Battle of France and Battle of Britain in 1940, over North Africa, the Mediterranean and the invasion of Soviet Russia – the scene of the most prolonged and brutal fighting of the war

Although dive-bombing was adopted by the United States and Japan the nations of Europe, other than Germany, were less inclined to embrace the tactic. However, under the terms of the Versailles Treaty of 1919, Germany was forbidden from producing any offensive warplanes, so Junkers Flugzeugwerke AG, arranged for its Swedish subsidiary, A B Flygindustri, based at Limhamn-Malmo, to build what was intended primarily as a two-seat fighter monoplane to meet a requirement of the Turkish government under the designation Junkers K 47.

Initially designed by Dipl Ing Karl Plauth, it followed the standard Junkers' practice of the period, of being built in parallel with an ostensibly civil counterpart, the A 48. In 1927 work began on the strut-braced, low-wing monoplane K 47 which featured two open cockpits for the pilot and gunner, twin fins to maximise the rearward field of fire, a fixed main undercarriage and a tailskid. However, on 1 November, shortly before flight testing began Plauth lost his life in a flying accident, so the design was completed after his death by Hermann Pohlmann. By the time the prototype was complete Turkey had lost interest, although the Soviet Union indicated some interest and so work continued. In the event, the Soviet government only purchased two or three examples, and the only operational use of the type was by China which bought twelve aircraft. Three were used by the *Reichswehr*'s clandestine test and training facility at Lipetsk in Russia and a small number of the unarmed civil version were purchased by the *Verkehrsministerium* (Ministry of Transport).

The situation in Germany changed rapidly after Adolf Hitler and the Nazis came to power in 1933. Hitler was determined to re-establish Germany's military might and had ambitions to create a brand new, modern air force, the Luftwaffe. Initially controlled by the *Verkehrsministerium* and later by the *Reichsluftfahrtministerium* (RLM – Reich Aviation Ministry) under Hermann Göring, the Luftwaffe remained a state secret until 1935, when it was publicly revealed to a stunned world.

Under the influence of Ernst Udet the World War I fighter ace and leading aerobatics pilot who became head of the RLM's Technical Office (responsible for the procurement of new aircraft designs), dive-bombing was adopted and in 1933 the Luftwaffe issued its first requirements for a specialised dive-bomber which eventually led to the Henschel Hs 123 biplane in 1936. The K 47/A 48 was also used in trials to investigate dive bombing: experiments that would be formative of Pohlmann's thinking in designing the Ju 87.

Although initially employed with great success during Germany's Blitzkrieg campaigns, the Ju 87's limitations were exposed during the Battle of Britain as, without local air superiority, the Stuka was found to be vulnerable to modern fighters. As World War II progressed and Germany was forced further and further onto the defensive, the Stuka's emphasis changed from dive-bombing to ground-attack duties where it suffered increasingly heavy losses. With no purpose-designed replacement available, the Ju 87 was forced to carry on for much longer than it should have done. Eventually superseded by the Fw 190, a few Stukas managed to fight on until the very end of the war in 1945, by which time its once feared reputation had long since evaporated.

Ju 87B-1, S2+AP of 6./StG 77 thought to have been crewed by the *Staffelkapitän* of 6 *Staffel, Hauptmann* Herbert Pabst and his *bordfunker* (radio operator/gunner) *Feldwebel* Woletz, about to take off for another sortie on the Eastern Front in late summer 1941. The aircraft was named *Anton der Zweite* (Anton the Second), written in white Gothic script on the cowling side, a possible reference to this being the second aircraft with the individual aircraft letter 'A' (Anton being the Luftwaffe phonetic alphabet name for A – which is just visible in white outlined in black on the yellow fuselage band), that the crew had flown in. Also of note are the original B-1 stub exhausts, the pair of SC 50 bombs under the wing and the 6./StG 77 'leaping bull' shield near the windscreen. The low contrast between the admittedly well-worn RLM 70 *Schwarzgrün* and 71 *Dunkelgrün* greens is well illustrated. *Author's collection*

Origins and Ju 87A

Even before the Hs 123 had entered service, the Luftwaffe began planning its replacement and in April 1934 an RLM specification was drafted for a new, two-seat, heavy dive-bomber. Four companies responded to this challenge including Junkers, who offered the Luftwaffe its new Ju 87 design. Following Karl Plauth's death, Hermann Pohlmann had continued the development of a dive bomber design, utilising the various A 48 airframes, fitted with dive brakes and powered by BMW 132 engines, which were initially tested at Junkers' factory at Dessau in Germany, before being moved to Sweden.

Ernst Udet, the notable World War I 'ace', who claimed 62 confirmed victories and was the highest scoring German fighter pilot to survive the war (and second only to Manfred von Richthofen), joined the Nazi Party in 1933 and became involved in the early development of the Luftwaffe, where he was appointed Director of Research and Development. He became a firm believer in the concept of dive bombing – apparently after flying an American-built Curtiss Hawk II, an export version of the US Navy F11C-2 Goshawk. However, other high ranking German officers, including Walther Wever (Chief of Staff of the Luftwaffe from March 1935) and Robert Ritter von Greim, (later to become a Luftwaffe general) both raised doubts about dive bombing following a daring demonstration by Udet, in May 1934, at the Jüterbog artillery range in one of the two Hawk IIs purchased by Germany, that such high-level nerves and skill could not be expected of average Luftwaffe pilots. Nevertheless, development of the dive bomber concept continued at Junkers and by the summer of 1934 a wooden mock-up of the Ju 87 had been built and inspected by a team of officials from the RLM, but no firm orders were as yet placed as there were several other contenders still in the field. Undeterred, Junkers commenced work on the first flying prototype in October.

Of immediately distinctive and recognisable form, the all-metal monoplane featured double-spar inverted gull-wings, of cantilever construction, incorporating Junker's arrangement of full-span, slotted flaps and ailerons which were hinged to the trailing edge. The wings also accommodated two large, sprung, fixed mainwheels protected by large 'trousered' fairings. Despite knowing that the Jumo engine planned to power the Ju 87 was still not ready, (the Junkers Jumo 10 in-line engine, later re-designated Jumo 210, was still in its early design

The Ju 87V4, *werknummer* 4924, in an overall natural metal finish, with black civil registration, D-UBIP on the wings and fuselage, and the black swastika on a white disc on a red band across the fin and rudder – one of the prototypes for the Ju 87A-0 series. *Author's collection*

stages), the company decided that the prototype should be fitted with a British-designed Rolls-Royce Kestrel V liquid-cooled, 640hp engine as a temporary solution. The Ju 87 V1 prototype, (later given the civil registration D-UBYR), first flew on 17 September 1935, from the Junkers factory at Dessau, fitted with the twin fin and rudder layout similar to the A 48, to give the rear-facing radio operator/gunner (who sat back-to-back with the pilot in a tandem cockpit) a clear field of fire with his single defensive machine gun. To ease construction Junkers arranged for the Ju 87's fuselage to be built in two halves that could be joined together along the centreline rather like a latter-day model kit. The maiden flight was successful and further prototypes were built, but during subsequent testing, when the V1 was put in to a 60° dive, the twin fin/rudder assembly broke away and the aircraft crashed killing test pilot, Wilhelm Neuenhofen and flight test engineer Heinrich Kreft. Consequently, the twin fin/rudder layout was abandoned and replaced by a stronger, single fin and rudder.

Construction of further prototypes went ahead, and an initial RLM requirement was placed in October 1935 for seven Jumo 210A-engined Ju 87A-0 pre-production aircraft. But, with the Jumo 210 engine still way behind schedule, Junkers began to consider using the Daimler-Benz designed DB 600 in-line engine instead. However, the Ju 87 V2, built from the outset with a large, square-profile single fin and rudder, received a German-designed BMW Hornet engine which quickly gave way to the 610hp Jumo 210A when it finally became ready for service following its prolonged development period.

Prior to commencing flight trials at the Luftwaffe's research facility near Rechlin, the second Ju 87 prototype, the V2, D-UHUH, was retrofitted with special slats under its wings outboard of its undercarriage fairings. These slats had been specially designed for dive-bombing and could be rotated downwards through 90° to act as dive brakes which would allow the aircraft to

Above: The twelfth production Ju 87A-1, *werknummer* 000023, finished in the RLM 61/62/63 'splinter' scheme, with RLM 65 *Hellblau* under surfaces, while still retaining the civil registration D-IEAU. In June 1938, this aircraft was the first production A-1 to be delivered to I./StG 162, when the unit started replacing its Henschel Hs 123s with Ju 87s. *Author's collection*

Below: The Ju 87A's Jumo 210 engine exposed during routine servicing by the groundcrew, nicknamed *schwarze-männe* (black men) by the Luftwaffe due their black overalls. Of note are the Anton's horizontal radiator shutters and stub exhaust manifolds.

Close-up of the nose area of a Ju 87A revealing the inboard located auxiliary undercarriage leg struts and the bomb trapeze crutch that swung down to ensure the bomb cleared the propeller arc. Of note are the engine cowling cheek-mounted oil cooler inlets and 7.92mm MG 17 machine gun in the starboard wing – only one wing-mounted gun was carried by the Ju 87A.

be more controllable as it dived. To further improve bombing accuracy the V2 was also fitted with an under-fuselage bomb cradle that was hinged to swing forward as the aircraft entered a dive. By doing so the cradle carried the bomb clear of the aircraft's propeller arc thus allowing it a free passage once released.

After successfully undertaking its maiden flight in February 1936, D-UHUH arrived at Rechlin for further trials and to compete in a fly-off against the other contenders for the RLM's dive-bomber requirement. These rivals included the Arado Ar 81 and the Blohm und Voss Ha 137. However, the real competition to the Ju 87 came from Heinkel's He 118 design with its powerful DB 600C in-line engine. As expected, both the Ar 81 and Ha 137 proposals were quickly eliminated from the contest but the He 118 continued to outperform the Ju 87 in nearly every criterion. The crucial test came when Ernst Udet himself opted to fly both candidates on dive-bombing trials. The Ju 87 performed well, if unspectacularly but for the He 118 the test was a disaster. Somehow the aircraft's controls seized up during its dive and although Udet managed to bail out before the He 118 crashed, all faith in the Heinkel product evaporated. Crucially Udet gave his backing to Junkers despite it being much slower and far less manoeuvrable.

Following Udet's lead, the RLM awarded Junkers with a contract to proceed with full scale development of the Ju 87 and a third prototype, the Ju 87 V3 was quickly produced. Although similar to its predecessors, the Ju 87 V3 introduced a simpler tail fin assembly and a slightly modified undercarriage assembly. Powered by the same Jumo 210A engine as the second prototype, the Ju 87 V3 took to the air for the first time at Dessau on 27 March 1936 whereupon it was transferred to Rechlin for additional trials. The fourth prototype, the Ju 87 V4, was finished to what the company expected production standard aircraft to resemble. As such it was built with an enlarged fin, a flatter engine cowling for improved forward visibility from the cockpit, straighter wing leading-edges and a fixed 7.92mm MG 17 machine gun in one of the wings. Still employing the Jumo 210A, the Ju 87 V4 first flew on 20 June 1936 and a few months later was modified with underwing slats for dive-bombing tests.

Ordered at the same time as the fourth prototype, the Ju 87 V5 was the first to make use of the DB 600 engine. Junkers still considered this Daimler-Benz product to be a possible alternative to its own Jumo design and was keen to establish the DB 600's performance criteria. After flying for the first time on 14 August 1936, the Ju 87 V5 went to Rechlin a few months later for an intensive series of flight trials. By this time an opportunity had arisen to test the Ju 87's capabilities in a combat environment by sending it to Spain where the Spanish Civil War had erupted.

(Backtracking only slightly, although the Ju 87 had been awarded an RLM order, a confidential directive issued by *Generalfeldmarschall* Wolfram von Richthofen on 9 June 1936 had called for the cessation of all further Ju 87 development. Udet immediately rejected von Richthofen's instructions and Ju 87 development continued. By 1936, Udet had, through his political connections, been placed in command of the *Technisches Amt*, the development wing of the RLM).

Spanish Civil War evaluation

The Jumo 210-engined V4 prototype, WNr 4924, D-UBIP, was transported in great secrecy to Spain on the Spanish freighter *Usaramo*, departing Hamburg on the night of 1 August 1936 and arriving in Cádiz on the 6th. With its civilian registration letters deleted, it was allocated the type code '29' and the individual aircraft number '1', and, like the Hs 123s sent to Spain with the Condor Legion, was somewhat bizarrely assigned to *Versuchsjagdstaffel 88* (VJ/88), the Legion's Experimental Fighter *Staffel*, initially formed to test the prototype Bf 109Vs and He 112Vs.

Probably still finished in overall natural metal, 29•1 took part in the Nationalist offensive, flying a total of 40 hours between December 1936 and January 1937, and making at least six dive-bombing sorties, but at some point soon afterwards, was returned to Germany. However, its overall combat performance was found to be wanting. Pilots complained that during a dive-bombing attack they were unable to get a clear view of their target through the Ju 87's sighting window in the cabin floor as it was liable to oil over, thus rendering the aircraft's bomb sight virtually useless. Flight characteristics were also criticised, many pilots claiming the Ju 87 was underpowered and was slow at climbing, especially when fully laden with fuel and a bomb. This lack of power made the aircraft difficult to recover from a dive after an attack and pilots regularly had to contend with gravitational forces as high as 6g. On one or two extreme occasions pilots even reported suffering momentary, but potentially fatal, blackouts while trying to pull the Ju 87 out of its dive.

After returning to Germany, the Ju 87 V4 was briefly replaced in Spain during the spring of 1937 by the Daimler-Benz powered Ju 87 V5 for comparative purposes. Then, in January 1938, three production Ju 87A-0s, powered by 670hp Jumo 210d engines, arrived in Spain, and were also allocated to VJ/88. Finished in the three-tone RLM 'splinter/segmented' camouflage scheme of *Dunkelbraun* 61, *Grün* 62 and *Hellgrau* 63 on the upper surfaces, and *Hellblau* 65 on the under surfaces, they were coded 29•2, 29•3 and 29•4, and had Spanish Nationalist saltire crosses and black disc markings applied.

During the first weeks of operations, further problems became evident, not least of which was that the aircraft's maximum bomb load of 500kg (1,102 lb) could only be carried if the gunner wasn't on board, other-

One of the three Jumo 210d-engined production Ju 87A-0s initially sent to Spain in January 1938, and allocated to *Versuchsjagdstaffel* 88 (VJ/88), the Condor Legion's Experimental Test unit. The Stukas soon adopted a badge comprising an umbrella and a bowler hat within a white diamond shape, (a play on the crew's pseudo-civilian status), only carried on the port undercarriage fairing. However, it was deemed inappropriate by higher authority, and replaced by the *'Jolanthe the Pig'* cartoon seen here on the port undercarriage fairing, which it is thought to have originated from the aircraft's ungainly appearance while taxiing over rough airfields, causing Stukas to be known as the *Jolanthe Kette*.

In the Spanish Civil War, much of the Condor Legion's aircraft servicing had to be done in the open air. A good shot for modelling super-detailers.

This page: Three close-up images of the nose and cockpit areas of various Ju 87As serving in the Condor Legion. The method of hinging the canopies is interesting in that the port, side panels and the 'roof' sections were designed to open whereas the starboard side panels were fixed. This sideways opening method was found to be impractical and was replaced by sliding canopy sections from the B-series onwards. Worthy of note are the transposed camouflage colours noticeable on the starboard mainwheel of the first two photos – possibly 29•5 (which replaced 29•4 after it was damaged) and 29•3.

Opposite page, top and centre: Two views of 29•3 being serviced 'somewhere in Spain', but thought to be La Cenia in 1938. What looks to be a 500kg SC 500 bomb can be seen on the ground under the aircraft's fuselage ready to be loaded on to the bomb rack trapeze crutch. Some of the slightly smaller 250kg bombs may be seen in the background. The Messerschmitt Bf 109 coded 6•42 in the background, was one of a batch of twenty-seven Bf 109Bs, (coded 6•19 to 6•45), fitted with VDM-Hamilton variable-pitch, metal, two-blade propellers that arrived in Spain in September 1937.

Below: A bombed-up Ju 87A-0 revving its 670hp Jumo 210d engine prior to another ground support sortie. However, during the first weeks of operations several problems became evident, not least of which was that the maximum 500kg bomb load could only be carried if the gunner wasn't on board, otherwise the bomb load was restricted to a 250kg SC 250 bomb.

Below: A Ju 87A-1 of *Sturzkampfgeschwader* 165 in the RLM 61/62/63 'splinter' upper surface scheme with RLM 65 under surfaces and the then new national markings, which re-introduced the *balkenkreuz* black cross outlined in white, on the fuselage sides and the upper and under surfaces of the wings. The black swastika (*hakenkreuz*) was retained midway across the fin and rudder, initially on a white disc over a broad red band, but later the red band and white disc were painted over in camouflage colours, dating this photograph to mid-late 1938. The first two characters of StG 165's *Luftkreiskommando* coding system, '52', can also just be seen. *Author's collection*

Opposite page, top: Close-up of what appears to be a 500kg SC 500 bomb loaded on the bomb crutch.

wise the bomb load was restricted to 250kg (551 lb). The large spatted undercarriage fairings were also found to have difficulty coping with the muddy springtime conditions found on Spain's primitive grass airfields which, reportedly, led to the spats having to be temporarily removed. Despite these operational concerns, the three aircraft supported the Nationalist forces, which included anti-shipping missions, until the autumn, during which time, after sustaining damage, 29•4 had been replaced by 29•5 (which may have been an A-1). All the Ju 87As were returned to Germany, as discreetly as they had arrived, in October 1938.

Pre-production aircraft

Meanwhile, while operational trials were being conducted in Spain, in Germany Junkers sought to act on the reports coming back from the fighting. The seven pre-production Ju 87A-0s the RLM had contracted Junkers to build alongside the planned prototypes during late 1935, were to be used for operational research purposes pending the official acceptance of the Ju 87 by the Luftwaffe. The initial A-0s, fitted with Jumo 210A engines, were delivered in May 1936, but, as the Ju 87 prototypes were already undergoing evaluation it was decided to delay the flight testing of the pre-production aircraft until the prototype tests were concluded. This postponement however did not deter the RLM from ordering a further four Ju 87A-0s during September 1936. The first seven A-0s had all been completed at Dessau by March 1937. Compared to the prototypes the pre-production aircraft had a much flatter engine cowling profile because their Jumo engines had been mounted in a lower position in response to complaints about poor forward visibility. Also, their rear fuselages had been set lower to provide the radio operator/gunner with a better field of fire for his single 7.92mm MG 15 machine gun. Straight instead of tapered wing leading-edges were also employed.

Trials of the Ju 87A-0 series, which commenced in December 1936, had shown that the aircraft lacked power in proportion to its size and weight, which reinforced the reports that later came back from Spain and forced Junkers to hurriedly retrofit all existing pre-production Ju 87s (together with the remaining prototypes) with a revised Jumo 210Ca engine. Rated at 640hp this new powerplant also featured a larger oil cooler inlet and had much superior coolant circulation systems.

The Ju 87A-0s were exclusively used for service trials and research. Much of the information they provided Junkers with was later incorporated into successive Stuka variants.

Ju 87A-1

Production standard Ju 87A-1s were first handed over to the Luftwaffe during the early part of 1937. Powered by Jumo 210D engines they were equipped with a two-position, adjustable Junkers H-PA-10 propeller for improved flight performance. Tests soon confirmed that the Ju 87A-1 could achieve a maximum speed of 180mph at an altitude of 13,123 feet and a range of 373 miles with a service ceiling of 22,966 feet under certain circumstances.

A plan to install two wing-mounted machine guns instead of the original single

weapon was abandoned due to weight problems so the Ju 87A-1 continued with a single MG 17 in its starboard wing and one rear-firing MG 15 in the cockpit for self-defence. For improved weapons delivery, a Siemens ETC 500/A bomb release mechanism (cradle) was introduced. This device could handle bombs weighing up to 500kg (1,102 lb) and typically the A-1 flew with either a single 500kg SC 500 or 250kg (551 lb) SC 250 bomb, however, as mentioned previously, the Ju 87A-1's radio operator/gunner had to be left behind, along with his MG 15, if a 500kg was to be carried. Clearly this was a major tactical weakness and left the aircraft exposed to attack from behind; consequently, the Ju 87A-1 frequently took to the air carrying a lighter SC 250 bomb and *both* crewmen!

To aid the Ju 87's pilot in the successful implementation of a dive-bombing attack, the A-1 introduced a new automatic dive recovery system (ADRS). This enabled the pilot to set up all the aircraft's control surfaces, trim settings and dive-brakes prior to commencing his dive. As the aircraft headed into wind (a necessity for dive-bombing operations) the pilot had to wait for his intended target to slide into view across the sighting window in the cabin floor. When it did, and having already set up the ADRS, the pilot pulled back on a lever which automatically deployed the Ju 87's underwing dive-brakes to their maximum extended position. This created immense amounts of drag, causing the Stuka's nose to want to pitch upwards except that an automatically activated trim tab on the elevators would lower to keep the aircraft level. The pilot would then put the Ju 87 into a dive during which he had to keep his intended target fully lined up on the centre of his bombsight. The Stuka's optimum diving angle was 80° and to keep the aircraft correctly positioned the pilot had to constantly monitor his angle of attack (AoA) using painted indicator lines on the inside of the cockpit canopy. As the Stuka dived it slowly built up speed, with an average descent of 8,000 feet being necessary to achieve the ideal velocity of 350mph. As the aircraft passed through a pre-arranged altitude mark, around 4,300 feet

Below: A pair of *Sturzkampfgeschwader* 165 Ju 87As being refuelled, probably at Kitzingen in Bavaria, where StG 165 was based in the late 1930s. The rather involved *Luftkreiskommando* military coding system comprising numerals and letters for unit and individual aircraft identification introduced in 1936 is visible on both aircraft, as are the transposed upper surface camouflage colours. Of interest, even at this early pre-war period is the camouflaged petrol bowser. *Author's collection*

From the summer of 1938 the Ju 87A began to be phased out from frontline units in favour of the much improved 'B' variant. The earlier variant remained relevant however, primarily as a trainer within the *Stukaschulen* where it saw several further years of service before finally being withdrawn in 1943-44. This particular example appears to have been repainted in the RLM 70/71 'greens' upper surface scheme, and has yellow outer under surface wing tips indicating service on the Eastern Front, perhaps in anti-partisan operations. It still carries its four-letter *stammkennzeichen* factory codes (ending in BV) under the wings.

above the ground, a warning siren would sound in the cockpit to alert the crew. Then at 2,300 feet the siren would cease which was the signal for the pilot to release the aircraft's bomb. Swung clear of the aircraft by its Siemens cradle, the released weapon would continue to fall along the Stuka's trajectory to its target. The ADRS would kick-in as soon as the aircraft's bomb was free and the system would automatically retract the under-elevator trim tab freeing the Stuka's nose to come back up again, thus forcing the aircraft out of its dive. As the Stuka pulled up, its pilot would retract the dive brakes and open the engine's throttle to commence his climb away from the target area.

Even with the ADRS, dive bombing in a Ju 87 required a high degree of skill and attention from the pilot, not to mention nerves of steel, and, in an age before the advent of G-suits, a cast iron stomach! It took months of careful training to produce a qualified pilot and it was perhaps no surprise that most Ju 87 crews regarded themselves as something of an elite force within the Luftwaffe, almost on a par with the 'glamour boys' flying fighters.

The A-1 was soon followed on the production line by the slightly revised Ju 87A-2 variant which incorporated larger undercarriage fairings, improved radio communications equipment, a tail fin that was slightly rounded off at the top and most importantly, a 680hp Jumo 210Da engine. This was fitted with a two-stage supercharger and drove a two-position Junkers H-PA-III adjustable propeller.

Production orders for both the Ju 87A-1 and A-2 began to be placed by the RLM from October 1936, even before the pre-production A-0 series had commenced testing. Junkers however was already at full stretch trying to meet the Luftwaffe's desire for Ju 52 transports and was additionally preoccupied with developing the new Ju 88 twin-engined medium bomber, so to help the company meet the RLM's order for Ju 87s the Weser Aircraft Company Limited of Bremen was brought in on a subcontract basis.

The first Ju 87A-1s entered service with the Luftwaffe during the spring of 1937 and were assigned to *I Gruppe, Stukageschwader 162* (I/StG 162 – i.e. 1st Wing, Dive Bomber Group 162). By the late summer of the following year, some 192 Ju 87As had been delivered by Junkers with 70 more coming from Weser.

Widespread usage

As more Ju 87s became available, the Luftwaffe was quick to re-equip and create new frontline units with them. After I/StG 162 had formed, additional Ju 87s were supplied to II/StG 162 at Lubeck-Blankensee and I/StG 165 at Kitzingen. IV(Stuka) *Lehrgeschwader 1* (IV(St)/LG 1) was created from I/StG 162, and served as a Tactical Development Wing to test the Ju 87 under operational conditions and devise appropriate new tactics. Also, to give as many of its crews as possible a taste of combat, the Luftwaffe regularly rotated personnel from Germany to Spain to fly the Ju 87's serving with the Condor Legion, where, operating under conditions of almost complete air superiority, the Ju 87As performed well although their flight capabilities were still relatively poor.

From the summer of 1938, the Ju 87A began to be phased out from frontline units in favour of the much improved 'B' variant. However, A-1s and A-2s still had a useful role to play as trainers and they enjoyed several more years' service in second line units before finally being withdrawn in 1943-44.

Ju 87B/C/R

Testing of the Ju 87 V2 and V4 prototypes had quickly shown that the Jumo 210 engine lacked sufficient power to make the Stuka a truly effective combat design. Studies directed at increasing the Jumo's output were therefore begun in late 1936 and by the spring of the following year Junkers had modified a single Ju 87A-1 at Dessau, with a completely redesigned fuselage, and powered by a 1,000hp Jumo 211A direct-injection engine which could drive either a Junkers H-PA or H-PC three-blade propeller. Re-designated as the Ju 87 V6, this aircraft undertook its initial flight on 14 June 1937 and immediately demonstrated a much-improved performance capability. A second Jumo 211A-engined prototype, the Ju 87 V7, flew in August of the same year and Junkers took this aircraft to act as the basis for an improved production model known as the Ju 87B.

The Ju 87 V7 incorporated a fully redesigned cockpit area complete with a new, two-section sliding canopy for easier access, and a single radio mast replacing the twin radio masts of the 'Anton'. The rear-firing MG 15 was retained but was now provided with a new circular, rotating lens-like mounting, which offered a greater field of fire. Additionally, instead of the original large undercarriage fairings, the V7 featured lighter, aerodynamically-shaped 'spats' which discarded the transverse strut bracing of the 'A' version's main undercarriage design, and were not only stronger but easier to maintain in the field. An enlarged fin and rudder was introduced to improve the pilot's control while the original ADRS was modified to include a speed monitoring device which maintained the aircraft's velocity at between 310 and 373mph during a dive. Finally, for improved ground strafing capabilities, the V7 was provided with a 7.92mm MG 17 in each wing.

Following on from the V7 came the generally similar V8 in November 1937 which in turn was followed three months later by the V9. These three prototypes provided the basis for six pre-production Ju 87B-0s which Junkers converted from existing Ju 87A airframes in 1938. After these, came the first production standard B-1s from an initial RLM order for 138 aircraft.

One of the Ju 87B prototypes, the V10, still in its overall natural metal finish and prior to its civil registration, D-IHFH, being added. *Author's collection*

This page: Two views of a newly completed Ju 87B-1, photographed at the Junkers airfield at Dessau. The aircraft is finished in the standard RLM 70/71 'greens' splinter scheme with small narrow bordered *balkenkreuze* in all six positions and the *hakenkreuz* placed centrally across the fin and rudder. Also of note is the relatively high upper/under surface demarcation line on the nose, a feature of early production Bertas. The large white numeral '29' on the rear fuselage is thought to be the 'last two' of the *werknummer*, (5029). The small white rectangle at the upper left of the fuselage cross is the clear perspex cover of the first aid compartment. *Author's collection*

Opposite, top: In January 1939, three Ju 87B-1s were sent to Spain and allocated to 5 *Staffel* of *Kampfgruppe* 88 (5.K/88). Finished in the recently introduced RLM 70/71 two-tone upper surface 'splinter' scheme with *Hellblau* 65 under surfaces, the usual Nationalist saltire crosses and black disc markings were applied. Powered by a 1,000hp Jumo 211A engine, the Bertas were cleared to carry a 500kg SC 500 bomb under the fuselage and four 50kg SC 50 bombs under the outer wings, as well as *both* crewmen.

Opposite, cente: At some point during early 1939, a further two (or three) B-1s joined 5.K/88 in Spain, as the unit appears to have operated at least five machines at any one time. 29•8, in the foreground, has had the Jolanthe the Pig cartoon applied to the port undercarriage fairing.

As Junkers was already preoccupied with other projects, the responsibility for building the bulk of the Ju 87B series passed to Weser Flugzeugbau GmbH's, (known as Weserflug), factories at Bremen and Berlin-Tempelhof. Early B-1s were recognisable by their simple exhaust stubs and fixed radiator cooling fairing, which were later superseded by far more effective ejector exhaust manifolds and hydraulically operated radiator cooling gills on later production aircraft. Until the arrival of the Ju 87B-1, Stukas operated by the Luftwaffe had been built with noise-making sirens in the upper leading-edges of each undercarriage leg. These operated by air passing through them at high speed (such as during a dive) to create a howling wail. However, during the production run of the B-1, special noise-making propellers, essentially propeller-driven sirens, with a diameter of 0.7m (2.3ft), nicknamed 'Jericho Trumpets', were fitted on the upper section of each undercarriage leg, activated by the pilot during a dive to emit an ear-piercing screech that was aimed at terrorising ground troops (and civilians alike) and weakening enemy morale. Once the attack was over they could be deactivated using oil-pressure switches.

Although the Jericho Trumpets added to the Stuka's psychological impact, they did have an adverse effect upon its dive speed and so were often deleted or isolated. In their place many Ju 87Bs began carrying bombs with small whistles attached to the fins, which produced a shrieking whine once released. As with the Ju 87A, the 'Berta' was initially restricted to a maximum 500kg (1,102 lb) bomb load although its additional engine power meant that the radio operator/gunner could be carried at all times – even with the SC 500 bomb. Performance-wise, the B-1 had a top speed of 242mph and a maximum range of 373 miles with a full weapons load, while its service ceiling was improved to a maximum of 26,250 feet.

The Berta's combat debut

Like earlier Stuka models, the Ju 87B-1 received its initial baptism of fire during the Spanish Civil War. Three aircraft were initially despatched to the Condor Legion in October 1938 and allocated to 5 *Staffel* of *Kampfgruppe 88* (5.K/88). Making their combat debut during the Catalonia Offensive in January 1939, they struck a Republican arms depot near Mayals and soon proved to be far more effective than the original 'Anton' series aircraft.

Finished in the recently introduced RLM two-tone upper surface 'splinter' scheme of *Schwarzgrün* 70/*Dunkelgrün* 71 with *Hellblau* 65 under surfaces, again with the usual Nationalist saltires and black disc markings applied, on 24 January, a formation of Ju 87Bs attacked the Port of Barcelona, in

concert with over thirty Heinkel He 111s. The Stukas were instrumental in the prevention of the destruction of a bridge near Barcelona by strafing the demolition engineers, although either return ground fire or the guns of a Republican Polikarpov I-15 fighter (sources differ), hit one aircraft wounding the pilot in the legs, and causing the aircraft to make a forced landing on the beach, which also injured the rear gunner.

At some point during early 1939, a further two (or maybe three – again references vary) B-1s joined 5.K/88, as the unit appears to have operated at least five machines at any one time, although it is difficult to be sure, as the aircraft weren't numbered consecutively – identified codes being 29•6, 29•8, 29•10, 29•11 and 29•13 – which may have been a ruse to purposely hide the true number of aircraft involved. The last attacks by Stukas were made in March, in direct support of the Nationalist advance on Madrid, then,with Franco's victory assured by the spring of 1939, the Condor Legion was recalled. Most of its aircraft were handed over to the victorious Nationalists, but the Ju 87 was considered too secretive to be left behind and all were returned, discreetly, to Germany during April 1939 aboard the freighter *Wilhelm Gustoff.*

The experience gained by Stuka crews in the Spanish Civil War proved invaluable, allowing them to perfect their skills under combat conditions, albeit that the Ju 87 had not been tested against a well-co-ordinated fighter opposition – that test was still to come!

Bottom: The Ju 87B was fitted with aerodynamically-shaped 'spats' instead of the 'Anton's large 'trouser' fairings, which were not only stronger but easier to maintain in the field. The 'Berta' also featured redesigned cockpit glazing, with a two-section sliding canopy for easier access. The rear-firing MG 15 machine gun was given a new rotating mounting which offered a greater field of fire. The Ju 87B, like 29•11 photographed here fully loaded with an SC 500 and four SC 50 bombs, helped the Luftwaffe to gain invaluable experience during the Spanish Civil War and allowed aircrew to perfect their skills under combat conditions, which they used to such devastating effect in the opening months of World War II.

Two photographs of a formation of three factory-fresh Ju 87B-1s, probably on a delivery flight (there are no rear gunner/radio operators aboard) to a Luftwaffe unit prior to the outbreak of World War II. All the aircraft have the *hakenkreuz* (swastika) in the central position across the fin and rudder and the small *balkenkreuze* at the extreme tips of the wings. The large white numerals on their rear fuselages are thought to be the 'last three' of their *werknummern*. Again, the high upper/under camouflage demarcation on the nose is noticeable. *Author's collection*

The success of the 'Berta' in Spain led the Luftwaffe to quickly re-equip its frontline units with the variant. By the late summer of 1939, Ju 87Bs were operational with I./StG 1 (at Intersburg), I./StG 2 (Cottbus), II./StG 2 (Stolp-Reitz), II./StG 2 (Langensalza), III./StG 51 (Wertheim), I./StG.76 (Graz), I./StG 77 (Brieg), II./StG 77 (Breslau) and IV.(St)/LG 1 (at Barth). The whole force was cleared to carry bombs up to SC 500 size. Additional contracts from the RLM eventually pushed the total number of Ju 87Bs on order from Weserflug, up to the 740 mark. In addition to this figure, a further 352 aircraft were ordered directly from Junkers, despite that company already being overworked. It was the RLM's intention to have 964 out of the 1,230 Ju 87Bs it had signed for in frontline use by July 1940. However, from June 1940, after delivering 311 B-1s, Junkers switched over to building the improved B-2 variant. This featured an uprated 1,200hp Jumo 211Da powerplant, hydraulically operated radiator cooling gills and strengthened undercarriage legs. The additional power available meant that the B-2 could carry up to a 1,000kg (2,205 lb) weapons load on a stronger centreline bomb cradle, in the form of an SC 1000 or its armour-piercing derivative, the SD 1000, and be fitted with two new, underwing ETC 50 VIIIa bomb racks which could accommodate 50kg (110 lb) SC 50 bombs. Weser also began building the Ju 87B-2 but all work on this variant drew to a close during 1941, when the much-improved Ju 87D model came into Luftwaffe service. By the time 'Berta' production ended, a total of 700 B-1s and 230 B-2s had been produced, with many of the surviving B-1s later being upgraded to B-2 standard.

Carrier-borne Stukas... the Ju 87C

Influenced by the Royal Navy's aircraft carriers, and (initially) by HMS *Courageous* specifically, Nazi Germany laid down a 28,090-ton carrier to be named *Graf Zeppelin* on 28 December 1936. This was to be the first of two such vessels intended to pioneer the *Kriegsmarine*'s (German Navy) use of aircraft carriers in support of their surface fleet, particularly (as then envisaged) for raids against enemy commerce on the Atlantic trade routes. (Apparently, the second carrier was to have been named *Peter Strasser*.)

It was intended that *Graf Zeppelin* would carry a contingent of twenty Fiesler Fi 167 multi-role attack biplanes, ten Messerschmitt Bf 109T fighters and a dozen Ju 87 dive-bombers. Operating the Stuka from a ship presented a whole new set of challenges for Junkers and the company began to devote considerable energy towards creating a 'navalised' variant of the Ju 87B. Two prototypes, the V10 and V11, B-0 airframes powered by Jumo 211A engines, were devised to act as development aircraft. Owing to delays, the V10 was not completed until March 1938, first flying on the 17th: the V11 flew for the first time on 12 May. Whilst the V10, WNr 4928, originally D-IHFH, but changed to *stammkennzeichen*, (the four-letter factory code), TK+HD, retained the Ju 87's standard fixed wing arrangement, the V11, WNr 4929, *stammkennzeichen* TV+OV, introduced a folding wing that would allow the variant to be more easily stored aboard an aircraft carrier. Both prototypes featured catapult-launch fittings and underfuselage arrester gear.

Both the V10 and V11 were undergoing flight trials by early 1938 without any noticeable problems, so Junkers set to work on producing the Ju 87C, (Cäsar in the Luftwaffe's phonetic alphabet), which was the designation of the production model for the *Kriegsmarine*. The Ju 87 V11 was brought up to full C-1 standard incorporating a fully jettisonable undercarriage in case of an emergency ditching in the sea, for which there were two inflatable 750 litre flotation bags in each wing and two 500 litre bags in the fuselage to enable the aircraft to remain afloat for up to three days in calm seas. In addition, the airframe was strengthened to absorb the shock of carrier landings, a manual wing folding mechanism was installed as was a quick fuel dump mechanism and deck landing arrester gear. Other special equipment included a two-man rubber dinghy with signal flares and survival rations stored inside the Stuka's rear fuselage section. By 15 December 1939, 915 arrested landings on dry land on a marked-out area, the same length and width as the *Graf Zeppelin*'s flight deck, had been made. The 'carrier Stuka' was to be built by Weserflug, at the company's Lemwerder plant, between April and July 1940.

During November 1938, 4 *Staffel*, *Trager-gruppe* (Carrier Group) 186, (4./Tr 186), was formed specifically to operate the Ju 87C on board *Graf Zeppelin*. However, as neither the ship nor the aircraft were yet ready for service, the unit initially operated a handful of Ju 87As from its base at Kiel-Holtenau. These were replaced in May 1939 by the more capable 'Berta' and a few of the first Ju 87C-0s to leave the Junkers factory. The Ju 87C had a take-off weight of 5,300kg

Showing the short exhaust manifold stubs of the Ju 87B-1 to good effect, this aircraft, which was photographed nosed over in soft ground at Prague-Ruzyne in Czechoslovakia in March 1941, was attached to *Fliegerführerschule* C12 (Advanced Training/Pilot Leader School 12), but is still carrying a badge that is thought to be of 7 *Staffel* StG 2 under the windscreen, presumably retained from its operational days. It was reportedly re-marked with factory *stammkennzeichen* codes NO+HP, possible after major servicing, and carried a yellow letter 'A' on the mid fuselage section.

(11,684 lb) and could be launched with an SC 500 bomb under the fuselage and four SC 50 bombs under the wings. The main production variant, the Ju 87C-1, was to have two MG 17s mounted in the wing with a MG 15 operated by the rear gunner.

In the event, *Graf Zeppelin* was never finished and lay uncompleted with further building work constantly delayed by Germany's need for other warships, and more importantly, submarines. On 6 October 1939, with the war already underway, 120 of the planned Ju 87Cs on order at that point were cancelled. Only a small number of Ju 87C-0s were ever delivered and, by May 1940, work on the definitive navalised Stuka, the C-1, had all but come to a standstill due to other more pressing priorities, consequently production of the C-1 was switched to the long-range version of the 'Berta', the Ju 87R. As for 4./*Tragergruppe* 186, it was eventually transferred to the Luftwaffe and was later elevated to form the basis of III./StG 1, as such it later saw much combat service during World War II.

Long-range Stuka

Operations over Poland and later Norway had shown that the Ju 87B's range was barely acceptable for combat missions especially within the context of a rapidly advancing Blitzkrieg assault. To extend the Stuka's combat radius therefore, Junkers quickly devised the Ju 87R-1 variant (the 'R' standing for *Reichweiteriausfuhrung* or Long Range Version, and 'Richard' in the Luftwaffe's phonetic vocabulary) at the beginning of 1940. Fitted with a pair of underwing-mounted 300 litre (66 gallon) drop tanks and enlarged internal fuel cells, each of which could house 240 litres (53 gallons), the Ju 87R-1 had a range of 780 miles

Two direct comparison views of the nose areas of the Ju 87B-1 and the Ju 87B-2 (or in this case the essentially identical R-2 as evidenced by the 300 litre drop tank under the wing). They show the difference between the shallower depth of the B-1's radiator intake to that of the deeper B-2/R-2's: different propeller blade shapes, that of the B-1 being the slimmer metal VDM product while the B-2/R-2 had a broader compressed wood Junkers VS 5 propeller; and the B-1's exhaust stubs compared to the ejector manifolds of the B-2/R-2.

(1,255km). Although it retained the same basic airframe of the 'Berta', the Ju 87R-1 was powered by the Jumo 211A although later variants had a choice of either the Jumo 211D, and later, the then brand new 1,410hp 211J engines. Like the 'Berta' before it, the R-1 employed the same standard communications gear of a FuG VIIIa radio for air-to-air and air-to-ground transmissions, an EiV-1a intercom link for crew communications and a Peil G-IV homing set. This latter piece of equipment enabled the Stuka to follow Morse signals, audio commands or its own flight instruments to reach a predetermined point. Also included was a FuG 25 transponder device.

The R-1 was followed by the R-2 variant, derived from the Ju 87B-2, and utilised the Jumo 211D engine. For operations over the Mediterranean a tropicalised variant, the Ju 87R-2/Trop, was produced featuring an engine dust filter and on-board desert survival equipment for its crew. After the R-2 came the Ju 87R-3, also powered by the Jumo 211D, but with improved air-to-air communications apparatus and tug-towing devices for hauling airborne gliders. Built only in small numbers, the R-3 was soon replaced on the production line by the Jumo 211J engined R-4. This had a redesigned mid-wing section housing self-sealing fuel tanks for improved protection against battle damage.

One hundred and five Ju 87R-1s were initially ordered by the RLM. Most were built by Weserflug (following the cancellation of the Ju 87C), and all had been delivered by the end of 1940, with the first examples joining I./StG 1 when it returned from Norway to participate in the final stages of the attack on France. While the R-1s were still being delivered, the first of a total of 471 R-2s began to enter service with the tropicalised R-2/Trop variant arriving from May 1941.

When the final Ju 87R-2 left Weserflug's factories in June 1941, production switched over to the R-4 variant. However, these were to be built at Berlin-Tempelhof and there was a subsequent delay in their delivery as Weserflug moved the necessary tooling over from its plant in Bremen. This holdup was later exacerbated by Allied bombing and the fact that the Luftwaffe urgently required its existing orders for the 'Berta' to be completed beforehand. Despite these procrastinations, a total of 145 R-4s were produced by October 1941 by which point the more advanced Ju 87D was ready for service (see Chapter 3).

The Stuka's reputation is born

On 1 September 1939, Germany invaded neighbouring Poland and two days later World War II began, as both France and Britain declared war upon Nazi Germany. For the Polish Campaign all of the Luftwaffe's existing Stuka units were deployed for action.

From airfields across East Prussia and North-eastern Germany the aircraft of I./StG 1, II. and III./StG 2, together with 4(St)/Tr 186, covered the *Wehrmacht*'s thrust into Northern Poland under the authority of *Luftflotte* 1 (Air Fleet 1). Elsewhere I./StG 2, III./StG 51, I./StG 76, I. and II./StG 77 with IV.(St)/LG 1 in support, attacked targets across Southern Poland under the command of *Luftflotte* 4. With little effective opposition from the Polish Air Force, thanks to the Luftwaffe's air superiority, the Ju 87s were generally able to operate unchallenged. Their choice of targets included vital communications centres, rail yards, key bridges, fortified defensive emplacements, artillery batteries and concentrations of Polish ground troops. An impressive degree of bombing accuracy was achieved, thanks to the Stuka crews' excellent training and in no small part to the fact that many of them had already seen action in Spain. This degree of precision, combined with the Ju 87's dreadful wail as it launched a diving attack created a fearsome reputation for the Stuka which the Nazi propaganda machine was quick to embellish. This hype was seized upon by the French and British media who ran lurid stories of Stukas strafing columns of Polish troops or defenceless civilian refugees with impunity. Thus the Stuka's renown was established across Europe.

Even the Luftwaffe began to believe that its Ju 87s were invincible. Only thirty-one Stukas were lost throughout the entire Polish Campaign and henceforth the use of dive-bombing was viewed by the German military as a decisive method of achieving success within the framework of their Blitzkrieg (Lightning War) philosophy. This whole tactic revolved around using fast-

Close-up of the Ju 87B-2/R-2's radiator intake showing the vertical radiator shutters, the broad compressed wood Junkers VS 5 propeller blades, and the ejector exhaust manifolds.

Top: A faked photo purporting to show a Ju 87B returning from a bombing raid on the Polish coastal region of Hela in September 1939 with its undercarriage sheered off after accidentally hitting the water when pulling out of a dive to thus 'emphasise' the strength and structural integrity of the Stuka. In fact, the aircraft were B-1s photographed over Spain, both with their undercarriages *intact*. The image was later doctored in which one set was eliminated and their Condor Legion markings carefully replaced by those of the Luftwaffe – note the orientation of the swastika on the far aircraft! The Luftwaffe Propaganda Kompanie (PK) is thought to have based the story on the real life experience of a 4.(St)/TrGr 186 Ju 87C-0, which was severely damaged by flak over Hela, forcing the pilot to jettison the undercarriage using the explosive bolts fitted to the C-0, prior to making a successful ditching in the sea. *Author's collection*

Centre: Ju 87B-1, A5+DH of I./StG 1, photographed around the time of the German invasion of Poland. I *Gruppe*, based at their forward base at Elbing in East Prussia, carried out the first bombing raids of World War II on 1 September 1939. This aircraft belonged to 1 *Staffel*, (identified by the 'H', the last letter of the code), and was marked with a white individual aircraft letter 'D' (white being the 1 *Staffel* colour) not only on the fuselage sides but above and below the wing tips, just inboard of the *balkenkreuze*. Just discernable beneath the windscreen is I *Gruppe*'s black 'diving raven' cartoon. *Author's collection*

moving armoured formations supported by long-range artillery and constant close air support (from Stukas) to smash through an enemy's weakest point. Once the break-through had been achieved the *Wehrmacht*'s elite Panzer Divisions were to race along behind enemy lines cutting their communications and supply routes, bypassing or isolating strongly defended positions to encircle vast numbers of troops while the slower moving infantry units dealt with the enemy's entrenched defences.

Stukas over Scandanavia

After conquering Poland, Hitler prepared to deal with France in the West, but first had to seize control of Denmark and Norway. Taking Denmark would give the Germans control of the Baltic Sea, whilst occupying Norway would guarantee a valuable source of mineral ores that were needed to fuel the Third Reich's war industries as well as opening up access to the North Sea and beyond that the Atlantic Ocean.

Codenamed *Unternehmen Weserübung* (Operation *Weserubung*), the attack on both these countries began in April 1940. The Ju 87s of I./StG 1 based at Kiel were tasked with providing dive-bomber support. Denmark fell easily but overrunning Norway proved more difficult as both Britain and France rushed troops to aid the collapsing Norwegian defenders. Unable to employ their preferred Blitzkrieg tactics the Germans had to rely on using *fallschirmjäger* (paratroops) and mountain troops to undertake much of the fighting until sufficient infantry forces could be airlifted in or despatched by sea to support the attack. Fortunately, the Luftwaffe was able to achieve air supremacy and was in a position to lend its not inconsiderable support to the fighting on the ground as well as challenging Britain's naval superiority in the North Sea. This prevented the Allies from adequately reinforcing or supplying their troops operating across Northern Norway and was a key factor in Germany's ultimate success.

The Stukas of I./StG 1 made their first telling contribution to *Weserburung* on 15 April 1940 when they attacked the radio station at Vigra, midway between Bergen and Trondheim. This facility was being used to organise the Norwegian defences and its destruction was considered to be of vital importance. Aware of this, the Stukas involved in the mission pressed home their attacks with such determination that one aircraft actually rammed the station's transmitter aerial to fatally disable it and prevent any further communications being made. On 19 April, I./StG 1 relocated to a forward operating base at Stavanger so that it would be much closer to the actual fighting on the ground and could provide much greater support. Later that same month the unit also began undertaking anti-shipping operations off the Norwegian coast. Attacking ships soon proved to be one of the Ju 87's greatest capabilities as dive-bombing was found to offer the best chance of scoring a direct hit against a moving vessel. Even if a ship attempted to take evasive action in open water a skilled Stuka pilot could usually manoeuvre his aircraft during its dive to keep the target in his sights until releasing his bomb. With a flight time on average of just five seconds the bomb would often strike the ship before it could change course again.

By the start of June 1940 I./StG 1 found itself operating out of Trondheim-Vaernes, although the fighting in Norway became something of a side-show due to events in the Low Countries and France which Germany had attacked the previous month. As Britain and France were preoccupied with events closer to home their defensive enclave around the Northern Norwegian port of Narvik was eventually abandoned. Alone, the Norwegians surrendered on 10 June, and the Germans imposed their own puppet regime under Vidkun Quisling.

Opposite, bottom: A pair of Ju 87B-1s, of II *Gruppe Stab*, StG 2, thought to be dispersed along the perimeter of their home base at Bonn-Hangelar, near Cologne, in early spring 1940 in similar conditions to those they would encounter during the invasion of France and the Low Countries in May. The nearest aircraft is T6+BC which, like the B-1 in the background, T6+AC, served with the *Stabskette* and as such both have the rather complex *Stab* II./StG 2 quartered coat of arms in a shield on their forward fuselages, made up of a red Brandenberg eagle, a black lion rampant, Austria's national colours, and a black cross with arms that have their ends indented in a shallow V-shape. II *Gruppe* StG 2 was unusual in that it operated independently from the rest of the *Geschwader* until January 1942 when it was absorbed in to StG 3, as III./StG 3.

Left: Ju 87B-2, T6+HL of 3./StG 2, is seen 'somewhere in France' in May 1940. It carries the original 3 *Staffel* badge (the arms of the city of Breslau) on a yellow disc adopted in April 1939 (seen below the windscreen) when the unit was formed from 3./StG 163 at Breslau – instead of the alternative but more familiar black Scottie dog on a yellow disc. The individual aircraft letter 'H' on the fuselage sides would have been yellow (the *staffel* colour) which was repeated on the front of the starboard main undercarriage spat. Just visible too is the yellow tip of the propeller spinner. The aircraft is loaded with SC 50 bombs under the wing: note how the *balkenkreuze* is painted over the dive brake.

Above: A formation of 5./StG 2's Ju 87Bs on a training flight in the winter of 1939/40 revealing virtually the entire airframe of *werknummer* 5486, T6+GN. The style of the individual aircraft letter 'G' is interesting.

Opposite page, top: A formation of Ju 87Bs of 5./StG 2 on a training flight over their home base of Bonn-Hangelar, near Cologne, in the winter of 1939/40. The rudder of the aircraft in the foreground carries *werknummer* 5486, identifying it as T6+GN once more. The aircraft beyond is WNr 5435 coded T6+KN, the propeller of which is interesting in that it appears to have a red tip with a thin white band, like the individual aircraft letter 'K' which is red with a white outline. The individual aircraft letter was invariably repeated above and below the wings, in black at this period, outboard of the *balkenkreuze*, as can just be seen on the wing tip at bottom left of the photo.

France and the Low Countries

On 10 May 1940, Germany unleashed its Blitzkrieg against the Low Countries (Belgium and the Netherlands), followed by a surprise thrust through the Ardennes region into Northern France itself. Nine *Stukagruppen* (Stuka Wings) were involved in this opening attack with a total of 320 Ju 87Bs and some thirty-eight Rs available. The Dutch and Belgian air forces were all but wiped out in the opening hours of the battle and those aircraft that did escape initial destruction were easy meat for the Luftwaffe's marauding Bf 109E fighters. Freed from the risk of interception, the Stukas roamed at will striking key targets as the *Wehrmacht* moved forward.

France's *Armée de l'Air*, although large in size, was mainly equipped with outdated aircraft that were little match for the Luftwaffe. Although the Royal Air Force's contribution of Hawker Hurricane fighters was more effective, it was too small and dispersed to have any significant impact on the air campaign and became hopelessly disorganised as the Allies retreated in the face of the Blitzkrieg. As the ground fighting swept through Belgium and Northern France, Ju 87s provided almost constant close air support to the fast-moving Panzer Divisions as they pushed ever deeper into enemy territory. So little and ineffective was the Allies' air opposition that just fourteen Stukas were lost in the first four days of the campaign.

The *Wehrmacht* achieved its crucial breakthrough by crossing the Rivers Meuse and Oise. These vital attacks were heavily backed by wave after wave of Ju 87s conducting pinpoint strikes against Allied defensive positions. Any attempt at a counterattack inevitably met with a horde of Stukas raining death and destruction from above. Seizing their advantage, the Germans stormed through the gaps in the Allied lines and raced for the English Channel hoping to trap a huge number of Allied units in the Low Countries. In fact, a mere fortnight after the German attack began, much of the British Expeditionary Force (BEF) had been forced to retreat to an enclave around the small port of Dunkirk, or face being encircled on the battlefield. Its only chance of survival was to be evacuated by sea to Britain. Amazingly, rather than let the *Wehrmacht* complete a valuable victory, Hitler, following a request by Göring, ordered the Luftwaffe to crush the BEF's enclave using airpower alone.

Operations over Dunkirk brought the Stuka into contact with large numbers of Hurricanes and Spitfires operating from secure airfields in Southern England for the first time. Although the German dive-bombers extracted a heavy price on British shipping off the Dunkirk coastline and caused losses amongst troops awaiting evacuation from the beaches, they themselves suffered quite severe casualties when caught by RAF fighters. It was a foretaste of the future, although few recognised the warning signs. Not unsurprisingly, the Luftwaffe alone could not prevent the evacuation from taking place and by the time it was concluded on 5 June 1940 over 330,000 Allied soldiers had been successfully rescued.

The Germans then re-grouped and turned their attentions towards capturing Paris and overrunning the remainder of France. Although worn out from their continuous operations over Dunkirk, the *Stukagruppen* hurriedly re-deployed ready to support the *Wehrmacht*'s attacks across the Rivers Marne, Seine and Loire.

Thoroughly demoralised, totally disorganised and heavily weakened from earlier battles, the French Army was unable to offer effective resistance. With the *Armée de l'Air* all but vanquished, the Luftwaffe's Stukas enjoyed a virtual carte-blanche over the

Left: Two views of what is thought to be F1+LL of 3 *Staffel*, I *Gruppe* StG 76, which was one of two of the unit's Ju 87Bs that was shot down while attacking Dunkirk on 27 May 1940. The badge on the cowling side is the so-called 'Syrian Panther' used by this single *Gruppe* unit that made up StG 76, (which was actually the Arms of Graz, in Austria, a white Griffon rampant on a green shield within a white disc). It is interesting to note that the fuselage *balkenkreuz* is still the pre-war narrow border style whereas the *hakenkreuze* is in the later, fully on the fin, position. The individual aircraft letter 'L' is in the 3 *Staffel* colour, yellow. Soon after the fighting in France had finished, II./StG 76 was re-formed as III *Gruppe* StG 77.

battlefield and again performed well. Paris fell, and on 22 June 1940, the French Government agreed to surrender.

Stuka's nemesis

With Northern France under German control and a puppet regime established in the south around Vichy, the Luftwaffe began to concentrate its units for the forthcoming assault on the British Isles. As a preliminary to any seaborne invasion it was deemed a priority for the Luftwaffe to defeat the RAF and establish air superiority over the Channel and southern England and negate the Royal Navy's dominance at sea.

The Stuka was viewed as a key component for the forthcoming air battle as its precision-bombing capabilities would make it an ideal platform for destroying the RAF's vital Chain Home early-warning radar stations along the South Coast or for striking against the airfields of Fighter Command throughout the Home Counties. Once the actual invasion had taken place, the Ju 87's role would be to support the *Wehrmacht*'s advance on London from a number of forward operating bases and also strike at any attempt by the Royal Navy to interfere with the German's sea supply routes. For the upcoming campaign the Luftwaffe gathered the whole of StG 1, StG 2 and StG 77 plus I./StG 3 with IV.(St)/LG 1 in support across Northern France and Belgium. These units could field around 400 Ju 87Bs and Rs.

The Luftwaffe's air offensive against the British Isles, so evocatively named the Battle of Britain by Prime Minister Winston Churchill, began in early July 1940, with a series of raids against supply convoys heading through the English Channel. The Germans believed that by attacking this shipping they could draw the RAF up to fight and destroy it en masse. The RAF refused to rise to the bait though and rarely committed more than a handful of their precious fighter squadrons at any one time. Consequently, the Stukas enjoyed a relatively successful spell, sinking a considerable number of merchant vessels. However, the warning signs that had first appeared over Dunkirk were quick to re-emerge whenever the RAF did intercept a Stuka raid, and, unable to match the performance of the RAF's Hurricanes and Spitfires, the Ju 87 suffered heavier than expected losses, and by the end of the month at least fifteen Stukas had been shot down.

On 8 August, the *Stukagruppen* conducted their first, large scale, co-ordinated attacks on a Channel convoy. An escort of Bf 109Es was provided but as the German fighter pilots had never escorted Ju 87s before, their tactics were poor and the RAF fighters were able to intercept the approaching Stukas with relative ease. Several of the Ju 87s scattered the moment the British fighters showed up but those that did press on were severely mauled and suffered substantial casualties. A few days later, on 12 August, the Luftwaffe launched *Unternehmen Adlerangriff* (Operation *Eagle Attack*), which was the start of its sustained campaign against the RAF's airfields throughout Southern England, with *Adler Tag* (Eagle Day), delayed by a day due to bad weather, to 13 August. The *Stukagruppen*, which were by now operating under the command of VIII *Fliegerkorps*, were tasked with the bombing of Middle Wallop airfield. En route to the target the massed Ju 87s were pounced upon by the Spitfires of No 609 Squadron and took a severe beating.

Two days after that, a 40-strong Stuka raid, this time with substantial fighter protection, managed to damage the airfields at Hawkinge and Lympne. The following day, the 16th, a similar attack was launched against RAF Tangmere but this was less successful and again and unacceptably high number of Ju 87s failed to return. Three days after this event, on 19 August, StG 77 was sent out to bomb the radar base at Poling but suffered a dozen or more losses. It was the final straw for the *Stukagruppen* – the lesson was clear – without total air superiority the Ju 87 was incredibly vulnerable to modern day fighters with no less than forty-seven having been shot down up to this point. Such heavy losses could not be sustained. While the rest of the Luftwaffe continued its offensive, the *Stukagruppen* were withdrawn from the battle: the Stuka's legendary reputation had been shattered.

This page: A Ju 87B-1, T6+JL of 3./StG 2, sporting the then new black Scottie dog on a yellow disc *staffel* badge introduced in 1940, (see photo of Ju 87B-2, T6+HL of 3./StG 2 for the alternative badge). Both T6+JL and the aircraft behind, T6+EL, still have the small, narrow-bordered *balkenkreuze* on the fuselage sides and at the extreme tips of the wings, and the *hakenkreuz* in the central position across the fin and rudder. The individual aircraft letters visible on the fuselage sides would have been yellow, (the *staffel* colour). A 500kg SC 500 and an 250kg SC 250 bomb lay on the ground.

Opposite page, top: A pair of Ju 87R-2s of 2./StG 3 seen flying over the harbour at Rhodes in the Aegean in early 1941 on a test flight (there being no *bordfunker*/gunner in the rear seat), probably from the unit's base at Trapani, Sicily. Still finished in the European Theatre RLM 70/71 'greens' upper surface camouflage scheme, neither aircraft, (S1+HK in the foreground and S1+AK) carry any unit badges, although S1+AK, thought to be the *Staffelkapitän*'s machine, has a white Mediterranean Theatre band around the rear fuselage, and a white 'fighter style' chevron on the fuselage side. Both aircraft are carrying 300 litre long range drop tanks.

The subsequent history of the Battle of Britain is well known. The Luftwaffe's failure to defeat the RAF led Hitler to first postpone and then abandon his plans to invade Britain. Instead, Germany's attention was being increasingly drawn to the East where the Soviets were ripe for attack, but the Stuka was already operating in sunnier climes...

Below: A *kette* of Ju 87Bs, possibly of 4./StG 2, escorted by a I./JG 27 Bf 109E-4, returning from a dive bombing sortie in Cyrenaica, in the eastern coastal region of Libya, in early 1941. Just visible on the leading Stuka's mid fuselage are traces of a white Mediterranean Theatre band, its position would indicate that it was painted around the area of the fuselage *balkenkreuze*. Also of interest is the individual aircraft identification letter 'C' (in the 4 *Staffel* colour, white, suggesting T6+CM would be its full code); the factory *stammkennzeichen* codes, ending in 'YL', were still carried under the wings, together with an additional letter 'A' towards the wing tip! *Author's collection*

Aobve: A trio of late production Ju 87R-1s of 6./StG 2, (the undercarriage spats of the furthest aircraft can just be seen under the fuselage of the middle machine) based at Ouilly-le Tesson, to the north of Falaise, France in the summer of 1940. T6+AP, the middle aircraft, is the *Staffelkapitän's* machine and carries the unit's early badge, a white Griffon rampant under the windscreen. The propeller spinner tips of both aircraft in the foreground are yellow (the *Staffel* colour) as is the individual aircraft letter 'A'.

Mediterranean strike

During January 1941, I./StG 1 along with II./StG 2 and the *Stab* (Staff) of StG 3 moved to Trapani on Sicily where they were placed under the command of X *Fliegerkorps*. The role of the Stukas was to support Germany's ally, Italy, in its struggle against the British in the Mediterranean and North Africa, by launching air raids against the Royal Navy and the island of Malta, which was proving to be a particular thorn in the side of the Axis. Their arrival was celebrated with an early success when, on 10 January 1941, a number of Stukas severely damaged the British aircraft carrier HMS *Illustrious*. The next day the cruisers HMS *Gloucester* and *Southampton* felt the Stuka's wrath whilst *Illustrious* was again damaged as she sheltered in Malta's Valletta Harbour.

Both I./StG 1 and II./StG 2 remained active over Malta and the Western Mediterranean throughout February 1941. However, at this stage of the war Germany had little interest in the Mediterranean and was busy preparing for its attack on Russia. These preparations were however about to be disrupted by events elsewhere.

A close up of what is thought to be S1+AK, the machine of the *Staffelkapitän* of 2./StG 3, seen in the previous photo on a test flight from the unit's base at Trapani, Sicily circa early 1941. The front of the propeller spinner is thought to have been white, (I *Gruppe* colour) with a red tip (2 *Staffel* colour). The individual aircraft letter 'A' was also red. *Author's collection*

The Balkans

Italy had attacked Greece from neighbouring Albania in 1940 in the hope of a quick and easy victory. The Greeks put up a surprisingly good opposition and forced the invaders back. Faced with a humiliating defeat, the Italian leader, Benito Mussolini, appealed to Hitler for German support. Germany could not afford to see its closest ally defeated, nor could it tolerate any instability within the Balkan region at a time when it was preparing to commit the bulk of its armed forces to an attack on the Soviet Union. Any unrest in the Balkans could easily be exploited by Britain and so Hitler reluctantly ordered his commanders to prepare plans for an invasion of Greece, as well as Yugoslavia where a pro-allied *coup d'état* had ousted the neutral Government.

On 6 April 1941, the Germans invaded Yugoslavia, as part of the Balkan Campaign (*Balkanfeldzug*) with the Stukas of I and III./StG 2 providing effective air support for the advancing ground forces along with I./StG 3. The outdated Yugoslavian Air Force could do little to stop the Luftwaffe and the Ju 87s were able to operate so freely that they even participated in the bombing of the capital, Belgrade.

After overwhelming Yugoslavia, the Germans rolled on into Greece under the code name *Unternehmen Marita* (Operation *Marita*). This time the Greeks were unable to repel the invader despite being reinforced by large numbers of British and Commonwealth troops transported from North Africa. With defeat a certainty, the Royal Navy began evacuating allied forces to the island of Crete on 24 April. Three days later Athens fell and by the close of the month the whole of the Greek mainland was under German control.

Above: A Ju 87R of 1./StG 77, S2+DH, caught on film in what the Luftwaffe termed a *kopfstand* (head stand or nose over) or maybe more sarcastically, *Flieger Denkmal* (Airman's Monument), at its forward landing ground base at Le Mesul-Angat, in Normandy, after returning from an attack on the radar base at Poling, West Sussex, on 19 August, when StG 77 suffered over a dozen losses.

On 20 May 1941, StG 2's aircraft were called upon to support the massive German airborne invasion of Crete, code-named *Unternehmen Merkur*, (Operation *Mercury*). Although the attacking German *fallschirmjäger* suffered heavy casualties, the Luftwaffe exacted revenge by bombarding Allied positions at will and striking at any Royal Navy warship operating off the Cretan coastline. In this latter role the Ju 87 again did well and Stukas claimed responsibility for sinking the British destroyers HMS *Kelly* and HMS *Kashmir* on 23 May. Two days later they struck again and sank the cruiser *Gloucester* and the destroyer HMS *Greyhound* while also damaging the aircraft carrier HMS *Formidable*. By the time Crete fell on 31 May 1941, Luftwaffe *Ju 87s* alone had sunk over 120,000 tons of allied shipping.

Barbarossa

Hitler's long planned invasion of the Soviet Union finally commenced on 22 June 1941 under the code name *Unternehmen Barbarossa* (Operation *Barbarossa*). The bulk of the Luftwaffe was deployed to support this mammoth endeavour and seven *Stukagruppen* (under the authority of II and VIII *Fliegerkorps*) were provided to perform close support missions.

As in previous German invasions, the Luftwaffe easily achieved air superiority over the large but mainly obsolete and ill-prepared Soviet Air Force (*Voyenno-Vozdushnye Sily*, VVS). Many of the VVS's aircraft that did manage to avoid being destroyed on the ground during the opening hours of the assault were shot down by Luftwaffe fighters. With the threat of interception all but gone, the *Stukagruppen* were once again free to back-up the advancing *Wehrmacht* formations and, just as in the Polish Campaign, the Ju 87 enjoyed a relatively trouble-free period of bombing and strafing Soviet ground forces.

Such was the demand for air support from the *Wehrmacht* during the first few weeks of *Barbarossa* that the Luftwaffe was unable to divert its Stuka units to other duties such as anti-shipping missions. However, in September 1941 attacks were launched against the Soviet Black Sea and Baltic Fleets. These early anti-shipping operations achieved some success, notably by damaging the Soviet battleship *Marat* as it lay in harbour at Kronstadt in the Gulf of Finland that served as the base of the Baltic Fleet. A follow-up strike a few days later saw one Stuka pilot, Hans-Ulrich Rudel – who would later go on to become one of the Luftwaffe's most experienced and highly decorated Stuka pilots – achieve fame by dropping a single 1,000kg (2,205 lb) SD 1000 bomb on the crippled *Marat* causing its fore end to blow up and rendering it a constructive total loss

Left: Luftwaffe *schwarze-männer* groundcrew crank up the engine of a *Stab* II./StG 77 Ju 87B-1 via the oval slot in the port side cowling. Other points of interest include the *Stab* II./StG 77 badge, (a black lion rampant on a yellow and red shield), the oil and octane warning triangles either side of the badge, the port wing mounted 7.92mm MG 17 and the siren propeller mounted on the undercarriage legs. The yellow cowling would indicate that the aircraft was involved in the Balkan Campaign against Yugoslavia and Greece dating the photo to around April/May 1941.

Top: A Ju 87B-2 thought to have initially served with I *Gruppe Trägersturzkampfgruppe* 186 in 1940, hence the numbers on the cowling and the mainwheel spats, which was a feature of that unit, although confusingly, the numbers do not match – the numeral '9' on the cowling probably being the original, in red with a white outline, while the numeral '32' on the mainwheel spat looks as if it has just been hastily applied. It may well be that the aircraft was photographed later in its service life, while operating with III./StG 1 which was formed from I./TrG 186, in the Balkans in the summer of 1941, and the light patch just visible on the rear fuselage may well be a yellow Eastern Front Theatre band. If so, the aircraft would almost certainly have carried the *Geschwader* code 'A5' but still retained the numerals as individual aircraft identification.

Centre: A fully-armed Ju 87B-2, S1+FK, of 2 *Staffel* StG 3, possibly on its way to bomb Tobruk in the autumn of 1941. The white Mediterranean Theatre rear fuselage band appears to have been applied at a slight angle and the RLM 70/71 'green' upper surfaces have faded in the harsh Libyan sun. Although the bombs under the wings are standard German SC 50s, the one under the fuselage appears to be an Italian 250kg bomb with the metal ring around the fins.

Above: A desert-camouflaged Ju 87R-2 at a forward landing ground in Italy, possibly on a delivery flight to one of the North African-based Stuka *Gruppen* in what appears to be RLM 79 *Sandgelb* upper surfaces with RLM 80 *Olivgrün* patches. The aircraft is still carrying the factory applied *stammkennzeichen* codes, KP+MP, which would indicate that it has been camouflaged during manufacture rather than overpainted in service, although the exhaust staining seems heavy.

(though not sufficiently 'total' to prevent its aft end from being used as a gun platform).

Additional anti-shipping missions succeeded in destroying the Soviet cruiser *Kirov* and damaging the battleship *October Revolution*. However, these achievements were not without a price. For example, Hauptmann Ernst-Siegfried Steen, the vastly experienced Commanding Officer of III./StG 2 was killed while attacking the warships of the Baltic Fleet and many other highly skilled Stuka crews were lost in similar raids. Likewise, up and down the Eastern Front, an increasing number of Ju 87s succumbed to Soviet anti-aircraft fire as they flew ever more demanding bombing missions over the frontline. Then, as the autumn of 1941 gave way to one of the harshest winters on record, the German ground offensive slowed to a crawl. Soviet resistance stiffened and with Moscow in its sights the *Wehrmacht* ran out of steam. The Luftwaffe too was suffering. Operating from poorly prepared ex-VVS airfields that became clogged with mud in autumn then froze hard during the winter months, it was all but paralysed and could no longer provide the support so desperately needed by the hard-pressed ground forces.

On 5 December 1941, the Soviets launched a surprise counter attack around Moscow and immediately drove the *Wehrmacht* back. Unable to rely on air support the Germans nearly collapsed, but rallied at the last moment and blunted the assault. When the front stabilised again, in January 1942, it had become clear that the glory days of the Blitzkrieg were well and truly over.

Return to the Mediterranean

During December 1941, *Luftflotte* 2 was hurriedly transferred from the Eastern Front to the Mediterranean, taking with it the Stukas of I and II./StG 3. The role of the Ju 87s would be to support the Axis ground campaign in North Africa where Germany had again been forced to intervene to aid her Italian ally. In January 1942, a third *Gruppe* was added to StG 3 (III./StG 3) as the Axis forces under General Erwin Rommel drove the Allies back across most of the territory they had taken from the Italians in 1940-41. This fast-moving offensive was heavily supported by StG 3's Stukas who particularly distinguished themselves for their role in the capture of the important fortress of Bir Hakim from the Free French. Ju 87s also participated in the bombing of the strategically vital port of Tobruk during June 1942, as Rommel's troops headed for the Egyptian border, and the little-known town of El Alamein where the Allies were preparing their final defensive positions. By this point, StG 3 had started to re-equip with a new sub-type of the Ju 87, the Ju 87D 'Dora', which offered an improved performance over the 'Berta'.

Below: A Ju 87R-2 taking off from what appears to be an Italian airfield, with other Ju 87s dispersed along the runway.

Bottom: A Ju 87R-2, individual aircraft letter white 'B', possibly of 1./StG 77, being re-armed on what appears to be an Italian airfield with Messerschmitt Bf 109Es dispersed along the flight line, the one on the left with a chevron and vertical bar marking of a *Gruppe* Adjutant in front of the fuselage cross.

Ju 87D/G

In the spring of 1940, Junkers had begun studying ways of redesigning the Ju 87 to take advantage of the new 1,400hp Jumo 211J engine, complete with supercharged intercoolers. Taking into account the improvements introduced by the 'Berta', a new variant known as the Ju 87D (Dora) was introduced. This was immediately recognisable from its predecessors by its refined nose profile and aerodynamically re-profiled cockpit canopy.

To improve the Stuka's defensive capabilities, the original single rearward firing MG 15 machine gun was replaced by a twin 7.92mm MG 81Z weapon, while additional armour protection was added around key sections of the aircraft. The Ju 87D also introduced a new, re-designed undercarriage unit, with smaller, more streamlined spats, that was, as with earlier Stuka variants, fully interchangeable with wheels or skis. However, due to initial problems with localised weaknesses in the new landing gear forks and mainwheels, many of the initial production Ju 87D-1s were completed with the legs and spats from the Ju 87B-2. For emergency crash-landings, Junkers intended that the new undercarriage should also be completely jettisonable by means of small explosive charges. However, these proved far more difficult to develop than had first been anticipated and were not cleared for operational use until the start of 1944.

With larger internal fuel tanks and a built-in ability to carry two underwing drop tanks, the Ju 87D-1 had an increased flight time of 2 hours 15 minutes. It also boasted a considerable increase in offensive capabilities by being cleared to carry a single 1,800kg (3,968 lb) SC 1800 bomb below its fuselage. Alternatively, a 1,400kg (3,086 lb) SD 1400 or 1,000kg SD 1000 could be employed instead, along with two 500kg SC 500 or four 50kg SC 50 bombs beneath its wings. Production problems with the Jumo 211J again led Junkers to consider alternative powerplants and for a time the Daimler Benz DB 603 engine was seen as a viable option. However, trials with this proved disappointing and the idea was abandoned late in 1941.

The two initial 'Dora' prototypes, the Ju 87 V21 and V22 had both flown by February 1941. A third prototype, the Ju 87 V23, was the first to take to the air using a DB 603 for power and this was followed in May 1941 by the Ju 87 V24 which was configured as a 'tropicalised' variant (later being designated as the Ju 87D-1/Trop).

The first Doras

The first production 'Doras', the Ju 87D-1 series, entered Luftwaffe service during the spring of 1942, and initially went to I./StG 2 on the Eastern Front. The next unit to re-equip with the type was StG 77, while from May 1942 a number of D-1/Trop deliveries were made to StG 3 in North Africa. The D-1 was soon followed by the Ju 87D-2 which featured a stronger tailwheel unit, improved armour protection and onboard glider towing equipment, although it was only built in small quantities and soon gave way to the Ju 87D-3.

By this point in the war a certain malaise had settled across Germany's aviation industry and production rates had fallen quite dramatically despite increased combat losses. Stuka production for example had dropped to just 476 aircraft per year but the introduction of the 'Dora' saw this figure rise rapidly to 917 by the end of 1942.

The third Dora prototype, Ju 87V23, *werknummer* 0540, *stammkennzeichen* SF+TY, used for intensive testing initially by Junkers and then at Rechlin for the official RLM tests during the spring and summer of 1941. It was fitted with a Jumo 211J engine within a more streamlined cowling, and featured a re-designed and more aerodynamic canopy glazing and slimmer, more aerodynamic main undercarriage legs and spats. Initially the D-series retained the 45ft 3in wingspan of the previous B-series…

... which were lengthened to 49ft 2.5in on the D-5 and subsequent sub-types converted from the D-5 such as the D-8 and G-2, as seen on this example which may be a G-2 judging by the lack of wing armament. Both *author's collection*

The Ju 87D-3

This variant was specially configured for ground-attack work. It incorporated extra armour along its vulnerable under fuselage section, around vital engine cooling components and most importantly of all, close to the cockpit, to shield the crew from small arms fire. An adverse effect of all this additional protection though was an increase in weight, so to help compensate for this the D-3 became the first Stuka variant to be built without 'sirens' fitted.

Co-produced initially alongside the Ju 87D-1, the D-3 later became the standard production model and spawned a dedicated torpedo-bomber model known as the Ju 87D-4. This could be fitted with either a 750kg (1,653 lb) or 905kg (1,995 lb) aerial torpedo for anti-shipping duties and also featured two wing-mounted 20mm MG 151/20 cannon instead of the usual MG 17 machine guns. Each cannon had a magazine capacity of 180 rounds. However, by the time it was ready for service, the need for a dedicated anti-shipping Stuka had passed. Consequently, only three examples of the D-4 variant were ever delivered to the Luftwaffe and these were later reverted to D-3 specification.

The Ju 87D-5

Probably the definitive Stuka variant was the Ju 87D-5. Rather than being an out-and-out dive-bomber, the D-5 was intended from the outset to act as a ground-attack aircraft as, by mid-1943, the Luftwaffe's operational requirements turned from offensive strikes to providing close air support to the hard-pressed *Wehrmacht*. As a result of this switch of emphasis, the D-5 was the first Ju 87 variant to be produced without dive brakes. It was also the first to be cleared to use the jettisonable undercarriage system, although in reality this was rarely employed. Despite being based upon the preceding Ju 87D-3, the D-5 introduced longer span wings for better flight handling as well as pioneering the use of mass-balanced ailerons. It also made use of extensive armour protection and benefited from an increased flight endurance thanks to its larger 480 litre (106 gallon) internal fuselage tank and two 150 litre (33 gallon) wing fuel tanks. Underwing 300 litre (66 gallon) drop tanks could also be carried. For ground attack purposes, the D-5 incorporated wing-mounted 20mm MG 151/20 cannon but retained the rearward firing twin 7.92mm MG 81Z machine guns. In its underfuselage ordnance cradle it could carry a single bomb – ranging from the 250kg (551 lb) SC 250 up to the mighty 1,800kg (3,968 lb) SC 1800 – and its underwing racks could handle SC/SD 50 or larger SC 70 bombs along with the new range of SD 1/SD 2 cluster munitions which were carried in either AB 250 or AB 500 containers.

Entering service during 1943, the Ju 87D-5 quickly became the most common Stuka variant of the mid-war period. It was planned to be followed on the drawing board by the generally similar D-6 with simplified electrical systems, a revised bomb release mechanism and other minor alterations. However due to Germany's worsening situation and a shortage of raw materials the D-6 was never actually produced. Instead Junkers began converting existing

Top: Intimate view of a derelict Ju 87D-1 or D-3's 1,400hp Jumo 211J engine, exposed and being inspected by British Commonwealth service personnel 'somewhere in North Africa' probably in late 1942. Also of note is the canvas gaiter covering the oleo suspension scissors of the Dora's slimmer main undercarriage leg and the shape of the more aerodynamic wheel spats. Initially the D-series retained the wing-mounted 7.92mm MG 17 machine gun in the faired housing and the mounting for the siren propeller, which seems to have only been fitted to D-1s and early production D-3s.

Bottom: Classic image of a Ju 87D-3 entering a dive. Although the unit can't be identified, the aircraft's individual aircraft letter is 'B', and is thought to have been operating on the Eastern Front and as such the band around the rear fuselage would have been yellow. The aircraft is fitted with the fairings, and the wind-driven siren propellers, and carries a single SC 250 bomb under each wing. *Author's collection*

Opposite page, top: A Ju 87D-5, showing what appears to be the remnants of a well-worn temporary white winter scheme on the cowling top, armed with SD 50 bombs under the wings, fitted with whistles on their fins, and an AB 500 containing anti-personnel bomblets under the fuselage centreline. Possibly photographed in the late spring of 1944 on the Eastern Front, the long barrels of the wing-mounted 20mm MG 151 cannon identify the aircraft as a D-5. *Author's collection*

Ju 87D-1s to a new specification, the Ju 87D-7. This involved adding the lengthened wings and MG 151/20 cannon armament of the D-5 variant together with a new 1,500hp Jumo 211P engine with special exhaust damper pipes for night attack operations. The closely related Ju 87D-8 was merely a conversion of the existing D-3 with the same features as the D-7 except that it had no flame dampers and was intended to complement the Ju 87D-5 on daylight ground-attack missions.

The tide turns...

By February 1943, two key battles had turned the tide of World War II against Nazi Germany. Firstly, in North Africa, the British 8th Army had broken Rommel's forces at the Battle of El Alamein (23 October to 11 November 1942), forcing Rommel to begin a long retreat. The Ju 87s of StG 3 did their best to stem the British breakthrough but the RAF had control of the air and the Stukas paid a heavy price for their efforts. As Rommel withdrew, the Luftwaffe was forced to flee too. By November 1942, StG 3 was down to just thirty operational aircraft and could make little effective contribution to the fighting. To make matters worse for the Axis, a combined Anglo-American invasion force, Operation *Torch*, landed in Morocco and Algeria and opened a second front. Although Axis reinforcements flooded in to establish a bridgehead in Tunisia StG 3's cause was not helped by the fact that one of its airfields at Djedeida was overrun by the Allies and over twenty of its Stukas were captured intact. As a result of this catastrophe, StG 3 was withdrawn from the North African Theatre at the close of 1942 to re-equip.

The unit returned to Tunisia with a fresh consignment of Ju 87s just in time for a renewed allied offensive. Flying from bases around Bone, StG 3 suffered more losses in the face of growing allied air power and was again forced to withdraw, in May 1943. As the last remaining Axis units in North Africa surrendered, StG 3 took up a new home on Sardinia and Sicily to again re-equip, with Ju 87D-5s. Eventually the unit was relocated to the Eastern Front as the Luftwaffe finally accepted that the Stuka was a virtual 'sitting duck' in the face of superior Anglo-American aircraft.

The Eastern Front

It was on the Eastern Front that the second blow to Germany's chances of winning the war came. During the summer and autumn of 1942, the *Wehrmacht* had launched a major offensive across southern Russia that had quickly become concentrated into a titanic struggle for the city of Stalingrad. The Luftwaffe's *Stukagruppen* played a key role in supporting the *Wehrmacht*'s Sixth Army as it advanced towards this objective and even participated in the bombing of the city itself. However, the Russians resisted every step of the way and clung on to a tiny bridgehead in the ruined city just across the wide River Volga. Thousands of Red Army reinforcements were ferried daily across this waterway to prevent the Sixth Army from taking complete control of Stalingrad, and every day the Luftwaffe's Stukas pounded the vulnerable Soviet vessels as they struggled to get through, but once the fighting around Stalingrad degenerated into small-scale urban warfare there was little the Stukas could do to aid German troops. The onset of winter again severely curtailed the Luftwaffe's operations and the *Stukagruppen* could only look on helplessly as the Russians launched a counter attack which quickly encircled the Sixth Army.

Despite an ambitious, and ultimately futile, attempt to re-supply the trapped German forces by air and a brave relief effort by *Generalfeldmarschall* Erich von Manstein, one of the *Wehrmacht*'s best military strategists, the Sixth Army was doomed. Its pitiful remnants finally capitulated in February 1943 and, for the first time along the Eastern Front, the Soviet Army had decisively halted then crushed a major German offensive.

After Stalingrad the Russians pressed on and attacked the important industrial city of Kharkov. The Stukas of II./StG 1, the whole of StG 2 together with I. and II./StG 77, were called in to stop the advance. But heavy losses during the previous year's fighting and a lack of spares meant that the *Stukagruppen* had

Above: A Ju 87D-3, of 7./StG 1, whose *Staffel* badge it carries on the cowling side and is therefore probably coded J9+NH, photographed returning at low level from a sortie on the northern sector of the Eastern Front with empty bomb racks. Casting its shadow on the steppe below, the aircraft is fitted with a fairing for the Wind-driven siren propeller and has the appropriate yellow band around the rear fuselage.
Author's collection

A Ju 87D, *werknummer* 2705 (see number on the fin top) – either a D-1 or an early D-3 as it is fitted with the fairings and propellers of the sirens on the undercarriage legs – of *Stab* I./StG 2 over the Eastern Front in 1942. Coded T6+SB, it carries the I *Gruppe Stab*'s black Scottie dog on a green disc outlined in white, just in front of the windscreen. The propeller spinner tip is also thought to be green. The I *Gruppe* identification letter 'B' appears to be white which is an unusual, if not a completely unknown variation, generally the colour was black like the *Geschwader* codes (it being more usual for the individual aircraft letter to be 'coloured') and is applied over the standard Eastern Front yellow rear fuselage band. The other non-standard marking is the white numeral '2' on the wheel spat, which may be a temporary tactical marking or may serve to identify the *Gruppenstab* 1a Operations Officer.

Opposite page: Three photographs of what appear to be different Ju 87G-1s. All have fairings for wing-mounted armament which would indicate they were modified from Ju 87D-3s. Fitted with Bordkanone BK 37, 37mm anti-tank cannon, based upon the earlier Rheinmetall 37mm Flak 18, these self-contained gun pods each had two six-round magazines firing armour-piercing tungsten carbide-cored ammunition at a cyclic rate of 160 rounds per minute. *Author's collection*

few aircraft available and they were unable to make much of an impact. In February 1943 Kharkov fell although a brilliant counterattack by von Manstein retook the city and stabilised the front again during March 1943. During this assault the Ju 87s of StG 2 and StG 77 were again much in demand.

By the late spring of 1943 it was becoming clear to many Luftwaffe commanders that the Ju 87 was fast becoming outdated and could no longer adequately provide the ground-attack support demanded by the *Wehrmacht*. Its potential replacement, the Henschel Hs 129, soon proved to be far from suitable as it lacked power and manoeuvrability, thus the Luftwaffe had no option but to continue using the Stuka until something better came along. Where that successor was to come from nobody knew, for no design requirements had yet been properly issued to the German aviation industry.

As mentioned earlier, by this point in the war the *Stukagruppen*'s emphasis had moved from pure, high-level dive-bombing, to shallow diving or low-level ground attacks – both of which were far less accurate or effective in terms of results achieved. The switch was not only due to Germany being forced increasingly on to the defensive but also because of mounting losses among experienced Stuka crews. These casualties could not be made good by the Luftwaffe's inadequate training system and those new crews who did join the frontline units often lacked the necessary tuition to properly implement dive-bombing or shallow attack techniques. Hence, because of the urgent need to overcome Allied superiority in troops, tanks and artillery, (especially on the Eastern Front), Junkers sought to develop a dedicated ground-attack/tank-busting version of the Stuka that could operate alongside the Hs 129, which eventually resulted in the Ju 87G 'Gustav'.

The 'Gustav'

The Ju 87G-1, based upon the D-1, first flew in January 1943 and was armed with a pair of underwing mounted 37mm Flak 18 cannon especially for use in the tank busting role. These powerful weapons each had a magazine containing of six, solid-shot, armour-piercing rounds that were designed to penetrate up to 120mm of armour before exploding.To cater for the increased weight of the Flak 18, the G-1 had its wing mounted MG 17s deleted but kept its rearward firing MG 81Z for self-defence. The underwing cannon also made the G-1 far less manoeuvrable and much slower than any other version of the Stuka making it a great deal more vulnerable to enemy fighters or ground fire. Equally, the very nature of anti-tank operations exposed the Ju 87G to enormous danger. An attack upon an armoured formation required the Stuka to fly at very low-level and ideally at an angle-of-attack of 60 degrees with the pilot opening fire from just 200 yards, preferably aiming at a tank's weaker topside armour or its less-weak side or rear. This left the aircraft more susceptible to ground fire. Despite these risks the Luftwaffe's need for 'tank-busters' was so urgent that it had no choice but to accept the Ju 87G into service.

Production of the Ju 87G-1 commenced in March 1943, utilising converted Ju 87D-3 airframes, and after initial trials one of the first operational 'Gustavs' was used in action on the Eastern Front for the first time in May 1943. On that occasion, Stuka 'ace' Hans-Ulrich Rudel flew the aircraft over the Kuban Bridgehead in the Crimea. Despite the G-1's sluggish performance and poor handling, Rudel managed to destroy several Soviet T-34 tanks and his success encouraged the Luftwaffe to begin re-equipping part of StG 2 with 'Gustavs' in time for the forthcoming Battle of Kursk.

The Battle of Kursk

Codenamed *Unternehmen Zitadelle* (Operation *Citadel*), the Battle of Kursk in July 1943 was the last throw of the dice for the Germans on the Eastern Front. Over 900,000 German troops, supported by 2,700 tanks and 10,000 artillery pieces were to be employed to cut off a large salient around the small town of Kursk. The Luftwaffe mustered over 2,000 aircraft to support the attack with the Stukas of III./StG 3, all of StG 2 (including the newly formed 10.(Pz)/StG 2 with 'Gustavs' under the command of Hans-Ulrich Rudel) and the whole of StG 77 providing ground-attack cover.

The Russians had anticipated the German move though, and had gathered over 1,300,000 men with 3,300 tanks and 20,000 artillery pieces to defend the salient. In the air a rejuvenated VVS could call upon 2,000 aircraft including many of the new Yak and LaGG fighters that were a match for anything the Luftwaffe had.

When the German assault began on 5 July, it met dogged resistance from the start. While the 'Gustavs' concentrated upon destroying Soviet armour (Rudel himself

Centre: The Ju 87G-1, was the first sub-type to be armed with this weapon, although Hans-Ulrich Rudel, the well-known Stuka ace, had suggested using two 37mm Flak 18 guns after achieving success against Soviet tanks with standard wing-mounted 20mm MG 151/20 cannon, and as a trial, a pair of these gun pods were fitted to Ju 87 D-1, WNr 2552. With Soviet tanks the priority targets on the Eastern Front, the development of a production variant as a successor to the Ju 87D began in November 1942 and the first flight of the Ju 87G-1 took place on 31 January 1943, and by April, the first production Ju 87 G-1s were being delivered to frontline units.

Bottom: Nicknamed *Kanonenvogel* (cannon-bird), BK 37-armed Ju 87s proved spectacularly successful, especially in the hands of experienced Stuka pilots such as Rudel, and many had a white *Panzerknacker* (tank buster) symbol stencilled on the cowling. Some 230 Ju 87Gs were built – the G-1 converted from D-1/D-3 airframes which retained the standard span wing, but had the dive brakes removed. The G-2 was similar to the G-1 except for the extended wing of the D-5 series. The variant could also carry a 1,000kg (2,200 lb) bomb load. *Author's collection*

claimed a dozen T-34s on the opening day of the offensive alone) the more numerous Ju 87Ds sought to strike at Red Army lines of communications, artillery batteries and troop concentrations. They also proved to be useful minefield clearers by dropping bombs to detonate the thousands of anti-tank or anti-personnel mines sown by the Russians to blunt the German advance. However large numbers of Stukas fell victim to anti-aircraft ground fire or VVS fighters during these missions.

The decisive moment in the battle came on 12 July with a massive tank-versus-tank clash around the village of Prokhorovka. The Stuka played its part in this gigantic, swirling *mêlée* by raining bombs and cannon fire upon the Soviet armoured formations, but the Germans failed to achieve the decisive breakthrough they were hoping for and suffered heavier than anticipated losses both in the air and on the ground. The next day *Zitadelle I* was cancelled as news of an Anglo-American invasion of Sicily on 10 July led the *Wehrmacht* to divert a number of units from Russia to Italy.

A few days later, the Russians launched their own offensive around Orel. This was the first of many such attacks that slowly drove the Germans backwards. The Luftwaffe attempted to halt the Russian advances but it was being asked to do too much with too little and was continually paying a heavy price as more and more of its aircraft were lost.

By the late summer of 1943, Junkers had produced a refined variant of the 'Gustav', the Ju 87G-2 and eventually 210 examples of this were built. These enabled the whole of III./StG 2 to re-equip along with one dedicated anti-tank *Staffel* each from StG 1, 3 and 77.

Unit reorganisations

By late 1943, German forces were in retreat throughout Russia and Italy. During October, in recognition that the Ju 87's dive-bombing days were well and truly behind it, the Luftwaffe re-designated its Stuka units as *Schlachtgeschwader* (Ground Attack Groups) – so, for example, StG 1 became known as SG 1. Aware that the Ju 87 was obsolete and the pressing wartime situation meant that valuable resources could not be provided, the Luftwaffe finally decided to abandon any plans for a brand-new replacement for it. Instead an existing design, the Focke-Wulf Fw 190, was chosen for modification as a ground-attack aircraft. Not only was the Fw 190 much faster than the Ju 87, it was also more manoeuvrable and had an inherent air-to-air combat capability which gave it a chance of surviving one-on-one combat with an enemy fighter. Requiring only a single crewman, it also offered a degree of aircrew 'economy' given Germany's manpower shortage.

The first unit to receive Fw 190s was I./SG 5 (formerly IV(St)./LG 1). This unit had spent most of the mid-war period based in Norway where it had employed its Stukas on anti-shipping operations against Allied supply convoys sailing for the Russian port of Murmansk. Once I./SG 5 completed its conversion process in February 1944, the next unit to convert was III./SG 1 on the Eastern Front. As increasing numbers of Fw 190s became available, the Luftwaffe sought to rapidly convert its remaining *Schlachtgeschwader*. By November 1944 only III./SG 2 was left flying Ju 87s. This unit was now under the command of Hans-Ulrich Rudel who had been promoted to *Oberstleutnant* (Lieutenant-Colonel) shortly after recording the destruction of his 300th Soviet tank in a 'Gustav'.

A Ju 87D, either a D-1 or a D-3 of I./StG 1, thought to be flying over the Balkans in early 1943. It is fitted with the fairings, but no propellers in this instance, for the sirens on the undercarriage legs. The unit's black diving raven badge can just be made out on the cowling side and the Eastern Front yellow rear fuselage band is in place, although no codes can be discerned. The cylindrical shaped object under the wing is probably a *Mischlast Abwurbehalter* 250 (a mixed weapon load container), used to drop supplies to ground troops. Made of wood around a metal frame, these containers were parachute retarded. Note the light-coloured strip down the leading edge of the fin.

After the arrival of the Fw 190 in the ground attack role, many surplus Ju 87Ds were re-cycled at the Metallwerk Niedersachsen, Brinkmann und Mergell, Hamburg-Harburg based factory during late 1943/1944, with the standard span wing Ju 87D-3s re-designated as Ju 87D-7s (aka Ju 87D-3/Ns) and the longer span Ju 87D-5s as Ju 87D-8s (aka Ju 87D-5/Ns), powered by 1,500hp Jumo 211P engines and fitted with long pipe-like flame dampers over the exhausts. Extra radio gear such as the FuG 16z and FuG 25 were fitted and flash suppressors over the D-8's MG 151 cannon barrels, and in this configuration the aircraft were transferred to *Nachtschlacht-gruppen* (NSGr or Night Attack Wings), formed to undertake night harassment raids into enemy territory or support anti-partisan operations behind German lines. The *Nachtschlachtgruppen* performed surprisingly well right up until the end of the war. In all, seven units flew the Ju 87D in this role, not only on the Eastern Front but also in Italy, and this particular example, *werknummer* 141285, thought to be from 2./NSGr 10, coded 5B, with individual aircraft letter 'L' in red, was surrendered by its crew at Fürth in northern Bavaria, on 8 May 1945. Based at Wels in Austria, less than 320km from Fürth, the few aircraft still operational with 2 *Staffel* was all that remained of the *Gruppe* by May 1945. It is interesting to note that the aircraft had a yellow rudder and a yellow nose band (just visible on the original photograph) and a white spiral on what appears to be a black spinner.

Those Ju 87Ds ousted by the arrival of the Fw 190 were soon transferred to several *Nachtschlachtgruppen* (NSGr or Night Attack Wings). These had been formed to undertake night harassment raids into enemy territory or support anti-partisan operations behind German lines. Although limited in what they could achieve, the *Nachtschlachtgruppen* performed well and were a constant thorn in the enemy's side right up until the end of the war. In all, seven units flew the Ju 87 in this role, not only on the Eastern Front but also in Italy, and from late 1944 over Western Europe after the Allied armies came ashore at Normandy.

Trainers and experimental Stukas

In a bid to improve the Stuka's ground-attack capabilities, Junkers drafted plans for a new variant known as the Ju 87F. This was to be powered by a 1,750hp Jumo 213 engine and would feature a fully revised, strengthened airframe along with the increased span wings pioneered by the 'Dora'. As well as being armed with forward-firing MG 151/20 cannon, the Ju 87F 'Friedrich' was to also carry a dorsal barbette housing a single MG 151 and an MG 131 machine gun. The new model was to have a fully retractable undercarriage and was such a radical variation from the existing Stuka design that it was soon allocated a completely new designation – Ju 187. In theory, the new aircraft should have offered superior performance to the Ju 87D but experimental tests later suggested that this would not be so due to the Ju 187's increased weight, but before a prototype Ju 187 could be produced, the Luftwaffe decided to adopt the Fw 190 as its Stuka replacement and so the entire project was soon abandoned. What impact it would have had remains a matter for speculation.

To try and ease the difficult job of training new Stuka crews, Junkers also produced the Ju 87H dual-control trainer. Based on the 'Dora' but featuring an enlarged transparent blister along the rear canopy to provide an Instructor with a clear view ahead, the 'H' variant was to be built without dive-brakes and so its potential usefulness was immediately restricted. Additionally, building a dedicated conversion trainer diverted valuable resources away from the production of badly needed Ju 87Ds so the 'H' (Heinrich) variant was only ever manufactured in small quantities. After the initial H-1, Junkers produced the Ju 87H-3 and H-5 versions which were based upon the D-3 and D-5 series respectively. The next training variant, the Ju 87H-7, was modelled on the D-1 but included the longer span wings of the D-5 whilst the final H-8 was created using repaired Ju 87D-3s that had been damaged in battle and were no longer considered suitable for frontline operations. These too were given the wings of the D-5 but had their armour protection considerably reduced to save weight.

End of the Stuka

Right up until Germany's final defeat in May 1945, diminishing numbers of Ju 87s remained in action with III./SG 2 and the *Nachtschlachtgruppen*, even though production of new aircraft had ceased during the autumn of 1944. The Luftwaffe even managed to form a fresh Stuka-equipped unit during January 1945, when I(Pz)./SG 9 was created by combining 10(Pz)./SG 1 and 10(Pz)./SG 3 into one unit. Using a mix of surplus Ju 87Ds and Gs, I(Pz)./SG 9 fought on along the Eastern Front until the bitter end. This new unit also had the honour of receiving one of the last Knight's Cross awards to be granted by the Nazi regime. On 1 April 1945, *Leutnant* Karl Spreitzer was decorated with this prestigious medal in recognition of his completing 652 operational sorties on the Stuka during which he was credited with the destruction of eleven enemy tanks.

Export Stukas

Despite its own pressing wartime needs, Germany felt obliged to support its allies throughout World War II by supplying them with aircraft including the Ju 87. Although the Luftwaffe's needs should have come first, many badly needed Stukas were instead diverted to Italy, Romania, Hungary, Croatia and Slovakia. Operated with mixed success, these aircraft would almost certainly have been better employed on the Eastern Front with the Luftwaffe but, as ever, political considerations came before military reality in Hitler's Third Reich. It was ironic therefore that some of the Stukas exported abroad were later involved in actions against the Germans as the tide of war turned in favour of the Allies.

Italy

In June 1940, Benito Mussolini jumped on Germany's bandwagon of success by announcing that Italy was at war with Britain and France. Although large, the *Regia Aeronautica* (Italian Air Force) was ill prepared for conflict and many of its aircraft designs were inferior to their British equivalents operating over the Mediterranean and across the North African Theatre. Italy thus turned to Germany for aid and in the late summer of 1940 the first Ju 87B-1/Trop examples were handed over.

These Stukas were first used in action against British targets on Malta during September 1940 followed by anti-shipping operations across the Western Mediterranean. The following month, Stukas based in Italian occupied Albania began raiding nearby Greece in support of the Italian Army's offensive there.

In North Africa, meanwhile, the Italians were forced onto the retreat across Cyrenaica by British and Commonwealth forces, so to reinforce its units fighting there, the *Regia Aeronautica* deployed the Stukas of its 96th *Gruppo Bombardemento A Tuffo* (Dive Bombing Attack Wing) in January 1941. Try as they might, the Italian Stukas alone could not halt their enemies and suffered surprisingly high losses.

Despite supporting Germany's invasions of Yugoslavia and Greece, Italy's attention was increasingly drawn to North Africa. Additional Ju 87s (including a few long-range 'R' variants) were donated by Germany between late 1940 and the summer of 1941 to allow the *Regia Aeronautica* to expand its dive-bombing operations but this growth was matched by ever-mounting losses at the hands of the British.

Following the decisive Battle of El Alamein in late 1942, Italian aerial activity across North Africa declined severely. By the time the Axis forces had retired to Tunisia, only the 101st *Gruppo* remained active with Ju 87s in the area as the *Regia Aeronautica*'s other Stuka equipped units were hurriedly withdrawn to rebuild themselves. By this time the more effective 'Dora' variant was entering Italian service and when the Allies invaded Sicily in July 1943, the Italians could call upon some forty-nine Ju 87Ds.

On 25 July 1943, Mussolini was overthrown and Italy began surrender negotiations. The following month the country capitulated and those areas under Allied control were declared Co-Belligerent. That portion of Italy still under German authority was occupied by the *Wehrmacht* which imposed a puppet Fascist regime to fight on. By this point only 121° *Gruppo* based on Sardinia was still operational with the Ju 87. At its peak the Stuka had been in use with seven *Gruppi* (Wings) of the *Regia Aeronautica* and over 200 examples had been delivered. Hearing of Italy's surrender, the 121st *Gruppo* switched sides en-masse to join the Co-Belligerent forces but its Stukas were little used and quickly became non-operational due to a lack of spares.

Romania

Another important German ally to receive the Ju 87 was Romania. The *Forţele Aeriene Regale ale României* (Royal Romanian Air Force, FARR), obtained its first Stukas during the summer of 1943 when the Ju 87D entered service. In all forty-five 'Doras' were handed over and these equipped *Grupul* 3° *Bombardement Picaj* (No 3 Bomber Group) which was comprised of *Escadrilla* (Squadrons) 73, 81 and 85. The unit first saw action over the Kerch Peninsular in Russia during July 1943. Although the FARR's Stukas performed well in combat it was not without a price. Within a month of commencing operations thirty-one out of the forty-five Romanian aircraft had been damaged in battle. Further active service across Southern Russia followed but *Grupul* 3° was increasingly forced to withdraw westwards to new bases as the Red Army advanced.

During May 1944, a second Romanian Ju 87 unit was created by the FARR when *Grupul 6° Bombardement Picaj* formed up with two squadrons (*Escadrillas* 74 and 87). It was later expanded by the addition of *Escadrilla* 86 and went into action in June 1944. While *Grupul* 6° bore the brunt of the FARR's Stuka operations *Grupul* 3° was temporarily withdrawn for re-equipping with 'Doras' after Germany agreed to supply Romania with 113 D-3s and D-5s. By August 1944 though, casualties had mounted in the face of growing VVS air superiority and the increasingly desperate nature of ground-attack missions the FARR was being asked to perform. *Grupul* 3° was down to just twenty-five aircraft of which only eighteen were serviceable while *Grupul* 6° reported losing twenty-eight out of its fifty-five Stukas.

On 23 August, a *coup d'état* overthrew the pro-Fascist regime in Romania and the country defected to fight alongside the Soviet Union. This move led the Germans to seize some of the FARR's aircraft including several Ju 87s but enough Stukas remained under Romanian control to go into combat against their former ally under the command of a combined *Grupul* 3/6 in Transylvania. By September 1944 most of Romania was in Soviet hands and *Grupul* 3/6 found itself supporting the Red Army's advance into Moravia and Slovakia. However, a lack of spares, combined with effective German AA and the Luftwaffe's still effective fighters took their toll amongst the remaining Romanian Stukas, and by the beginning of 1945 there was only enough aircraft left to equip one *escadrilla* so *Grupul* 3°/6° was disbanded. In its place *Escadrilla* 74 (a component of *Grupul* 8°) took over Ju 87 operations and continued to actively participate in operations against the Germans until the spring of 1945 when it began to convert to Soviet supplied aircraft.

Hungary

Another nation viewed as a key ally by Nazi Germany was Hungary. As early as 1940 a handful of Ju 87B-2s had been delivered to the *Magyar Királyi Honvéd Légierő*, MKHL (Royal Hungarian Air Force) which designated them as Ju 87K-2s. These were joined in March 1942 by a pair of surplus Luftwaffe Ju 87A-1s that had been retrofitted with Jumo 210D engines. Upon entering Hungarian service these aircraft were classified as K-4s. Both the K-2 and K-4 variants were assigned to Bomber Group 3/1 for training duties.

A dozen Ju 87D-3s and D-5s arrived in Hungary during the spring of 1943 where they were attached to the 2nd Dive Bomber Squadron. This unit first saw action with its Stukas over the Eastern Front in August 1943 when it was tasked with bombing suspected partisan bases near Bryansk. After this successful debut the squadron found itself serving with II./StG 77 and flew many missions alongside the German unit from its base at Poltava.

During March 1944, German forces marched into Hungary to prevent the country from negotiating a separate truce with the Soviet Union. With a puppet leadership imposed, the Germans then helped the Hungarians establish another Stuka unit, the 102nd Dive Bomber Squadron at Kolosvar. Initially equipped with ten ex-Luftwaffe Ju 87B-1s (known to the Hungarians as K-3s) this unit later received a dozen of the more effective D-5 variant. The 102nd Dive Bomber Squadron was quickly assigned to III./StG 77 and began combat operations in June 1944. The following month it was transferred to I./StG 77 and by August had undertaken forty-seven missions for the loss of four aircraft. It then moved to Hajduszoboszlo and thence on to Borgond where, in October 1944, most of its remaining Stukas were wiped out in an air raid.

Meanwhile the 2nd Dive Bomber Squadron had by now completed over 1,200 missions and had also recorded the somewhat rare achievement of shooting down two Soviet fighters with its Ju 87s. The unit had suffered a high percentage of losses though, with fifteen Stukas having been destroyed. With insufficient aircraft left to be effective and no new replacements on offer from Germany, the squadron was disbanded.

As the German puppet leader of Hungary, Admiral Miklós Horthy, began to recognise that defeat was only a matter of time, he secretly began talks with the Soviets about surrendering. A ceasefire was agreed but when it became public knowledge Horthy was overthrown by elements loyal to the Nazis who then invited Germany to occupy those parts of the country that were not already under Soviet control. While Horthy languished in jail, half his countrymen continued to fight alongside the Germans while the rest backed the Soviet Union. Despite the confused situation, the 102nd Dive Bomber Squadron nevertheless continued to fly alongside the Luftwaffe during the winter of 1944-45, by which time it had few Ju 87s left and so was re-equipped with Fw 190s.

Croatia

After occupying Yugoslavia in 1941, the Germans allowed a pro-Fascist leadership to be set up in the semi-independent republic of Croatia. The Croats proved willing allies and supplied a large number of troops to fight on the Eastern Front from 1943 onwards as well as establishing a small air force, *Hrvatska Zrakoplovna Legija*, (HZL, also known as the Croatian Legion). Using a mix of Luftwaffe aircraft, it was not until January 1944 that the Croats established their first Stuka unit when the Lucko Bomber Group was formed with a handful of Ju 87Rs and some ex-Italian Fiat CR.42s. This unit then served as the basis for a more permanent outfit which became known as 3 (Croat)./KGr 1.

During August 1944 Croatia's small number of Stukas went into battle against partisan forces operating under Joseph Tito in Yugoslavia. Based at Lubenstadt for the duration of these operations, the unit was eventually disbanded in October 1944 as Germany lost control of the Balkans.

Bulgaria and Slovakia

Two further countries received small quantities of Ju 87s – Bulgaria received twelve Ju 87Rs for training and perhaps thirty Ju 87Ds for anti-partisan operations in the summer of 1944. Slovakia received a few Ju 87Ds in 1943. (See page 45 for further details.)

Ju 87 Camouflage and Markings

Most of the prototype *Versuchs* machines were unpainted and left in a natural metal finish, with just the civil registration letters – 'D' (for Deutschland) followed by the aircraft's individual four-letter code, separated by a hyphen, such as the Jumo 210-engined V4 prototype, D-UBIP. This civil registration was invariably carried above the wings, the letter 'D' and the first letter of the individual aircraft registration, separated by a hyphen, above the port wing, with the remaining three letters above the starboard wing. The full registration, again with the 'D' separated from the other four letters by a hyphen, was also carried on both sides of the fuselage. A black swastika (*hakenkreuz*), the principal symbol of the German National Socialist Party, was applied midway across the fin and rudder on a white disc over a broad red band, with just a strip at the fin leading edge left bare. The aircraft's factory work number (*werknummer WNr*) was often applied in small black characters on the tailplane tips.

Spanish Civil War

As related earlier, the Ju 87 made its combat debut in 1937 with the Condor Legion during the Spanish Civil War, when the Jumo 210-engined V4 prototype, WNr 4924, D-UBIP, was sent to Spain, arriving in Cádiz on 6 August 1936. Assigned to *Versuchsjagdstaffel* 88 (VJ/88), the Legion's Experimental Test unit, it is believed that D-UBIP was still finished in overall natural metal, but with its civilian registration letters and swastika fin/rudder marking deleted. At some point it was allocated the Condor Legion code, 29•1, but as no photos appear to exist of it while operating in Spain, it is not known whether the code was actually applied to the aircraft or not.

In January 1938, three Jumo 210d engined production Ju 87A-0s were sent to Spain, and were also allocated to VJ/88. However, this time the aircraft were finished in the three-tone RLM 'splinter/segmented' camouflage scheme of *Dunkelbraun* 61 (dark brown), *Grün* 62 (green) and *Hellgrau* 63 (light grey) on the upper surfaces, and *Hellblau* 65 (pale blue-grey) on the under surfaces as introduced at the end of 1936 for all Luftwaffe bombers and applied on the production line. Under this factory-applied camouflage scheme, each aircraft type from each manufacturer had a different pattern (*Farben Sichtschutz*) for the sharp-edged 'splinter/segment' design, laid out on a grid pattern on factory camouflage paint drawings, and while a specific 'splinter/segment' design was used for each manufacturers' individual aircraft type, they were produced in two basic patterns, which were mirror images of each other and known as *Sichtschutzschema* A and B: i.e. Scheme A and Scheme B. Further, the RLM 61, 62 and 63 upper surface camouflage colours used in the Scheme A and the Scheme B patterns, could be, and were, often transposed, amongst the aircraft in a production batch, effectively giving up to six camouflage variations that could be applied to a particular aircraft type. The three Ju 87As sent to Spain were coded 29•2, 29•3 and 29•4, and had the aircraft type identification number '29' applied to the fuselage sides, separated from the individual aircraft number by a black disc. Like most of the other Condor Legion aircraft, the Ju 87As sported a white rudder with a black saltire cross and had black discs with white diagonal saltires above and below the wings, and white wingtips.

Originally, a badge with an umbrella and a bowler hat within a white diamond, outlined in black (a play on the crew's pseudo-civilian status), was painted on the outer face of the aircrafts' port undercarriage fairings. However, this was deemed inappropriate by higher authority and was replaced by a *'Jolanthe the Pig'* cartoon – the central character in a popular German animated film – which, it is thought, originated

Three production Ju 87As were sent to Spain in January 1938, and were coded '29•2', '29•3' and '29•4' and allocated to VJ/88. They supported the Nationalist ground forces until the autumn, during which time '29•4' had been damaged by ground fire over Bujaraloz and was replaced by '29•5', which is thought to have been a production standard A-1, as illustrated here. Finished in the three-tone RLM 'splinter/segmented' camouflage scheme of *Dunkelbraun* 61, *Grün* 62 and *Hellgrau* 63 on the upper surfaces, and *Hellblau* 65 on the under surfaces, all the Ju 87As had white rudders and black saltire crosses and the usual six Nationalist black discs, those above and below the wings with white saltire crosses, applied. Note the *'Jolanthe the Pig'* cartoon (the central character in a popular German animated film) on the port undercarriage fairing which it is thought to have originated due to the aircraft's ungainly appearance when taxiing over rough airfields, causing the Stukas to be known as the *Jolanthe Kette*.

One of the initial Ju 87A-0s sent to Spain in January 1938,'29•2' photographed at Calamocha in March 1937. Finished in the three-tone RLM 61/62/63/65 scheme with Nationalist markings, codes were positioned on either side of the fuselage disc. '29•2' initially carried the unit's original badge, an umbrella and a bowler hat within a white diamond shape outlined in black, (a play on the crew's pseudo-civilian status), on the outer face of the port undercarriage fairing, which was deemed inappropriate by higher authority, and replaced by the *'Jolanthe the Pig'* cartoon, seen on the previous photo of '29•5'.

from the type's ungainly appearance when taxiing over rough ground: henceforth the 'Stukas' were known as the *Jolanthe Kette*. One of the Ju 87s, 29•4, was damaged in the autumn of 1938, and was replaced by another aircraft which may have been an A-1, coded 29•5, and finished in the same three-tone RLM 'splinter/segmented' camouflage scheme.

The Ju 87As were returned to Germany in October 1938, by which time, home-based units were being equipped with the type, the first Ju 87A-1s entering Luftwaffe service during the spring of 1937. Initially assigned to I *Gruppe*, *Stukageschwader* 162 (I./StG 162 – i.e. 1st Wing, Dive Bomber Group 162), as more airframes became available, new units including II./StG 162 and I./StG 165 were formed, plus IV(Stuka) *Lehrgeschwader* 1 (IV(St)/LG 1) which was created from I/StG 162 and served as a Tactical Development Wing.

Luftkreiskommando

While still being finished in the factory-applied RLM 61/62/63 'segmented splinter' upper surface scheme with RLM 65 under surfaces, following a series of changes that came into force in the spring of 1936, new national markings were applied which included the re-introduction of a black cross outlined in white (*balkenkreuz*), carried on the fuselage sides at a mid-point between the wing and tail unit, and on the upper and under surfaces of the wings, initially placed near the wing tips. The black swastika (*hakenkreuz*) was retained midway across the fin and rudder on a white disc over a broad red band. At the same time, a rather involved system of military codes comprising numerals and letters for unit and individual aircraft identification was introduced that replaced the civil D-xxxx registration letters.

This new system consisted of five characters, two to the left of the *balkenkreuz* on the fuselage sides and three to the right. They were also applied under the wings, reading from the trailing edge, the first two under the starboard wing and the remaining three under the port wing, both sets positioned just inboard of the underwing *balkenkreuze*. As an example, taking an aircraft from StG 165, coded 52+C24 – the first numeral (5) identified the *Luftkreiskommando* (Local Air Command); the second numeral (2), the position of the *Geschwader* (Group) within the *Luftkreiskommando*; the letter (C), the individual aircraft within the *Staffel* (squadron); the third numeral (2), the *Gruppe* (Wing) within the *Geschwader*; and the fourth numeral (4), the *Staffel* within the *Gruppe*.

Two-tone green scheme

A new camouflage scheme was introduced during 1938 which was intended to be more suitable for the European environment than the earlier RLM 61/62/63 combination. Comprising just two colours, RLM 70 *Schwarzgrün* (black green) and RLM 71 *Dunkelgrün* (dark green), again in a straight-edged 'splinter' pattern, it was applied using factory paint charts that were also based upon a grid. Again, it allowed the two colours to be mirrored in A and B Schemes, and have the two colours transposed within the pattern. The under surfaces remained in RLM 65 *Hellblau* (light blue).

The three Junkers Ju 87B-1s initially sent to Spain in January 1939 were finished in this new two-tone RLM 70/71 green upper surface 'splinter' scheme and, like the earlier 'Antons', their rudders were painted white with black saltire crosses, had black discs on their fuselage sides and black discs with white saltires above and below the wings – and white wingtips. They too received the aircraft type identification number '29' on their fuselages which were separated from the individual aircraft numbers by a black disc. At some point during early 1939, a further two (or three) B-1s were sent to Spain and joined 5.K/88, as the unit appears to have operated at least five machines at any one time, although it is difficult to be sure, as the aircraft weren't numbered consecutively – identified codes being 29•6, 29•8, 29•10, 29•11 and 29•13 – which may have been done purposely to hide the true number of aircraft involved. All the B-1s were returned to Germany during April 1939.

The prelude to World War II

As a result of the Luftwaffe's massive expansion prior to World War II, it became apparent that certain administrative changes were called for, consequently, in February 1939, new *Luftflotten*, i.e. Air Fleets, were created. *Luftflotte* 1 encompassed Northern and Eastern Germany plus East Prussia; *Luftflotte* 2 took in North-West Germany; while *Luftflotte* 3 covered South-West Germany. In March of 1939, *Luftflotte* 4 was formed to cover South East Germany, Austria, and Czechoslovakia. Within each of the *Luftflotten* was a *Luftgau* (Air District) which took over the duties of the old *Luftkreiskommando*. These duties consisted in the main of administrative affairs. Operational functions were controlled within the *Luftflotten* by *Fliegerdivision* (Air Divisions). These were later renamed *Fliegerkorps* (Air Corps).

With the introduction of the new *Luftflotten*, a reorganisation of the structure of Luftwaffe units

The German military had a long tradition of using heraldic devices for unit identification and the Luftwaffe was no exception. It made widespread use of badges and emblems to identify either a *Staffel*, a *Gruppe* or a *Geschwader*, sometimes all three, which were generally applied on the forward fuselage of the aircraft. Most of the wartime Luftwaffe's badges, emblems or shields are known and identified, but this one on the nose of a Ju 87R-2, is a bit of a mystery. Thought to have been taken at Trapani, Sicily in early 1941, it shows what appears to be a red and black spider with a white cross on its back with a yellow and black striped worm in its jaws, all on a white shield. Badges and emblems were normally painted onto the airframe but this shield appears to be pasted on and as such *may* be spurious and simply used for propaganda or disinformation purposes. Looking at the non-Luftwaffe groundcrew filling the underwing 300 litre drop tank, the white cross on the spider's back might mean there is some inferred association with the *Regia Aeronautica* or indeed the Hungarian Air Force, both of whom were operating Ju 87s at the time.

was undertaken and a new coding system for bombers (including dive bombers) and all multi-engined aircraft, was devised that replaced the previous five-character codes with a four-character system. Introduced in the spring of 1939, almost on the eve of the outbreak of World War II, it was similar to the *Stammkennzeichen* factory codes, consisting of two characters either side of the fuselage *balkenkreuz*.

The wartime Luftwaffe code system

The new identification coding system was generally applied to the fuselage sides and wing under surfaces of all Luftwaffe bombers, including the Ju 87 dive bomber, transports, twin-engined fighters and reconnaissance/maritime/communications aircraft.

The first two characters invariably positioned to the left of the fuselage *balkenkreuz*, comprised a letter/number or number/letter combination, which identified the parent unit – usually the *Geschwader* (Group), or in smaller units the *Gruppe* (Wing). The next character immediately to the right of the fuselage *balkenkreuz*, and invariably painted in the *Staffel* (squadron) or *Stab* (Staff) colour, identified the individual aircraft within the *Staffel*, whilst the fourth and last character identified the *Staffel* within the *Gruppe*. A typical example to illustrate this practice: Junkers Ju 87B-1 of 1./StG 1, coded A5+DH.

A5 = *Stukageschwader* 1
D = Individual aircraft letter painted in the *Staffel* colour in this instance, white
H = 1 *Staffel* / I *Gruppe* identification letter

The colours introduced to identify the three *Staffeln* within each *Gruppe*, were white (RLM 21 *Weiss*) for the first *Staffel*, red (RLM 23 *Rot*) for the second *Staffel*, and yellow (RLM 04 *Gelb*) for the third *Staffel*, in which the individual aircraft letter would be painted or at least outlined in.

Although this colour coding system was used to designate the first, second, and third *Staffeln* within each *Gruppe*, the actual number of the *Staffeln* within a *Gruppe* could occasionally be higher, in which case other colours such as blue (RLM 24 *Dunkelblau*) and green (RLM 25 *Hellgrün*) – ostensibly *Stab* (Staff) colours – would often be utilised.

Generally, a *Stukageschwader* consisted of a *Geschwaderstab*, with three aircraft; three *Gruppen Stabs*, with three aircraft each; and nine *Staffeln* with between nine and twelve aircraft each. So, within a dive bomber unit, the aircraft complement was usually as follows:

3 aircraft	*Kette* (e.g. *Stabskette* (Staff Flight))
9-12 aircraft	*Staffel*
27-36 aircraft	*Gruppe* (e.g. of three *Staffeln*)
81-108 aircraft	*Geschwader* (e.g. of three *Gruppen*)

By September 1939, at the time of the German invasion of Poland, the Luftwaffe camouflage and markings changes were well in to the transitional period, with the majority of frontline aircraft sporting the new coding system, and either repainted or manufactured from new, like the Ju 87Bs and Rs, in the 'new' two-tone RLM 70/71 upper surface scheme.

BREAKDOWN OF *STAFFELN* AND *GRUPPEN*

Last Letter of Code	Individual Aircraft Letter	Colour
Geschwaderstab	A	Blue or Green
Gruppe I	B	Blue or Green
Gruppe II	C	Blue or Green
Gruppe III	D	Blue or Green
Gruppe IV	E	Blue or Green
Gruppe V	F	Blue or Green

Gruppe	I	II	III	IV	V
Colour	White	Red	Yellow	Blue	Green
Staffel	1	4	7	10	13 (White)
Last Letter	H	M	R	U	X
Staffel	2	5	8	11	14 (Red)
Last Letter	K	N	S	V	Y
Staffel	3	6	9	12	15 (Yellow)
Last Letter	L	P	T	W	Z

If more than fifteen *Staffeln* existed within a unit, they would receive the following letters:

Staffel	16	17	18	19	20

A new two-tone green camouflage scheme was introduced in 1938 which was deemed more suitable for a continental European environment and less time consuming to apply than the earlier RLM 61/62/63 combination. Comprising RLM 70 *Schwarzgrün* (black green) and RLM 71 *Dunkelgrün* (dark green) in a hard-edged 'splinter' pattern applied using rigid factory paint charts based upon a grid, the under surfaces remained in RLM 65 *Hellblau* (light blue). Ju 87B-1, T6+BC, photographed here at its home base of Bonn-Hangelar in the early spring of 1940, served with the *Stabskette*, and had the rather complex *Stab* II./StG 2 quartered coat of arms shield consisting of a red Brandenberg eagle, a black lion rampant, the national colours of Austria and a black cross. The individual aircraft letter 'B' was bright green (RLM 25 *Hellgrün*). Of note is the First Aid compartment access hatch adjacent to the top left angle of the fuselage cross.

Wartime national markings

Luftwaffe national markings also saw some changes during this period. Still consisting of the black *balkenkreuz* with a white border, but this was now thinly outlined in black, and varied in specific proportions and dimensions depending upon where it was positioned on the airframe – those above the wings retaining narrow white borders with thin black outlines, while those on the fuselage sides had much broader white borders, again outlined in black, while the *balkenkreuze* under the wings were of much larger dimensions, (a development learned from ground-to-air recognition problems in the Polish Campaign), with broad white borders, again thinly outlined in black.

The black *hakenkreuz* (swastika) on the fin and rudder lost its white disc and broad red band, and was simply bordered by a narrow white outline which also had a thin black outline, again in specific proportions and dimensions for individual aircraft types. Initially it remained placed centrally across the fin and rudder, overlapping the rudder hinge line – this central position being a left-over from the previous design – but was gradually repositioned fully on to the fin on new build aircraft during 1938/1939. On aircraft in service that still had the horizontal red band and white circle, invariably on the original RLM 61/62/63 finished aircraft, it was generally painted out, usually in RLM 61 *Dunkelbraun*, merely leaving a thin white outline to the 'arms' of the swastika, until the airframe was totally repainted in the RLM 70/71 scheme during routine servicing.

Generally, Ju 87s continued to operate in the RLM 70/71 upper surfaces with RLM 65 undersides scheme throughout the Battles of France and Britain and into the early months of 1941 on the Channel Coast and Norway, and it was only when Hitler decided to invade Greece and North Africa to prop up his Axis ally, Mussolini, that the Luftwaffe started applying tactical markings in earnest. Prior to this, propeller spinner tips had occasionally been painted in the *Staffel* and/or *Gruppe* colour and the under surfaces of a few Ju 87s undertaking night operations had been painted in a temporary coat of matt black.

North African and Mediterranean Campaigns

When the Stukas of StG 1, StG 2 and StG 3 transferred to Sicily in early 1941 to support the Italians fighting the British and Commonwealth forces in the Mediterranean and North Africa, they were still finished in the northern European RLM 70/71 'greens' scheme, but soon adopted white fuselage bands, like those carried by *Regia Aeronautica* aircraft, which became a form of theatre marking. The white bands varied in their widths and indeed their positions, sometimes being to the rear of the fuselage *balkenkreuz* and other times forming the 'background' to the cross, being the same width of the horizontal arms, but entirely circling the fuselage. Additionally, the under surfaces of the wing tips were occasionally painted white, but as with all operational units, variations and anomalies abounded.

It wasn't long before the Stuka units operating over the North African desert areas started applying a more suitable camouflage, initially using Italian paints like the sandy/tan *Giallo Mimetico* (Camouflage Yellow), painted in broad bands over the existing upper surface RLM 70/71. Occasionally the entire upper surfaces were overpainted in *Giallo Mimetico*, sometimes being left as a solid sandy/tan scheme, but at other times with a hard, or soft-edged mottle of *Verde Mimetico* (Camouflage Green). Later in the year and into 1942, when suitable supplies had arrived, German RLM 'desert' paint was applied, in

It wasn't long before Luftwaffe units operating over the North African desert areas started applying a more suitable camouflage. Initially Italian paints such as the sandy/tan *Giallo Mimetico* (Camouflage Yellow), were painted in broad bands over the existing upper surface RLM 70/71, but later, German RLM 'desert' paints were applied. It's difficult to tell in b&w photographs the source or origin of these 'desert' shades, but this Ju 87B, possibly from StG 3, (no unit badge or emblem is visible), appears to have overall sand coloured upper surfaces, possibly RLM 79 *Sandgelb*, with large areas of a darker colour, possibly RLM 80 *Olivgrün*, over it. A white fuselage band, like those carried by *Regia Aeronautica* aircraft and which served as the Theatre marking for Luftwaffe aircraft operating in the Mediterranean and North Africa too, can just be discerned on the fuselage, in this instance forming the 'background' to the *balkenkreuz*.

the form of a RLM 79 *Sandgelb* base, either left 'as is', or with a mottle of RLM 80 *Olivgrün*, either over the original RLM 70/71 scheme, or, albeit only on a relatively few machines, applied on the manufacturer's production line – later delivery replacement Ju 87B-2/trops and some early delivery Ju 87D-1/trops being finished in RLM 79 *Sandgelb* upper surfaces with RLM 78 *Hellblau* under surfaces.

As the ground war moved out of the desert regions of North Africa to the somewhat greener vegetation of Sicily, and then later to the Italian mainland itself, the Stukas reverted to the standard RLM 70/71 scheme, although later Ju 87D variants often had the so-called *westenmüller* mirror-wave/meander scribble pattern applied over the top, 'in the field', in light tans such as *Giallo Mimetico* or RLM 79 *Sandgelb*. The *westenmüller* was often applied over the national markings and sometimes the codes, especially the *Gruppe/Geschwader* codes and often the last (*Staffel* i/d) letter, just leaving the individual aircraft letter untouched.

The Balkan Campaign and Barbarossa

On 6 April 1941, the Germans invaded Yugoslavia, with the Stukas of StG 2 and StG 3 providing air support for the ground forces. Whereas Luftwaffe units operating in the North African theatre sported white identification markings, those used in the Balkans and Crete in 1941 adopted high visibility yellow markings, generally applied to the nose cowlings and rudders of the aircraft involved. It appears that no clear instructions regarding the extent of the areas to be painted yellow were issued as these markings varied on the Stukas from just a broad yellow band around the nose and underside radiator housing, to the whole of the engine cowling all the way back to the angled panel line: and from just the rudder, to the whole tail section including the fin and rudder and, in some cases, both surfaces of the tailplanes and elevator were painted yellow.

The invasion of the Soviet Union (*Barbarossa*) commenced on 22 June 1941, to which seven *Stukagruppen* were initially committed. As with the aircraft operating in the Mediterranean and North African Theatres, additional recognition markings were applied, and like those aircraft operating in the Balkans, yellow was chosen, this time in the form of a fuselage band, of various widths, positioned either to the rear of the fuselage *balkenkreuz*, or less frequently, in front of it, or occasionally forming the 'background' to the *balkenkreuz*, being the same width of the horizontal arms, but in all cases completely encircling the fuselage. Additionally, the under surfaces of the wing tips were invariably painted yellow.

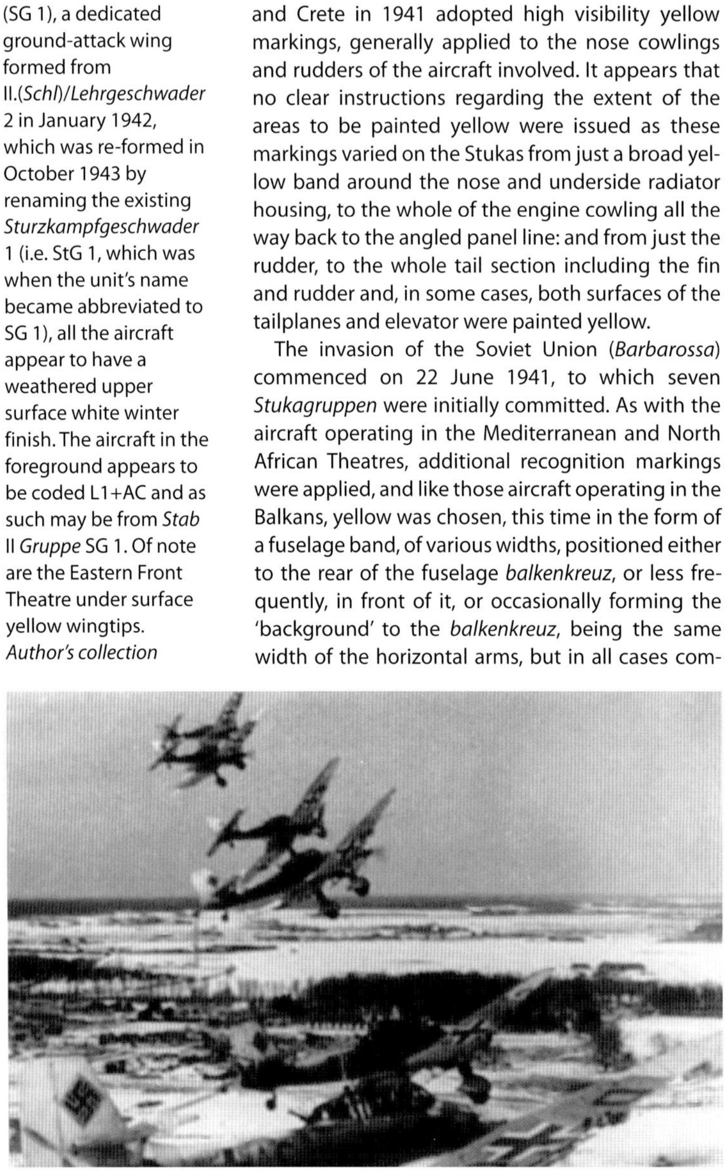

A mixed force of Ju 87D-3s and D-5s (see the difference in the wing spans), peeling off over a snow-covered area on the Eastern Front in the winter of 1943/1944. Possibly from *Schlachtgeschwader* 1 (SG 1), a dedicated ground-attack wing formed from II.(*Schl*)/*Lehrgeschwader* 2 in January 1942, which was re-formed in October 1943 by renaming the existing *Sturzkampfgeschwader* 1 (i.e. StG 1, which was when the unit's name became abbreviated to SG 1), all the aircraft appear to have a weathered upper surface white winter finish. The aircraft in the foreground appears to be coded L1+AC and as such may be from *Stab* II *Gruppe* SG 1. Of note are the Eastern Front Theatre under surface yellow wingtips. *Author's collection*

During the winter of 1941/1942, most Luftwaffe aircraft were overpainted on their upper surfaces in temporary white paint, (*Ikarin* A2515.21 or 7126.21), to help with camouflage in the snowy conditions. This was applied, either by paint brush or spray gun, in either a solid coat or a mottle of various densities. By whatever method the 'snow scheme' was applied, it weathered quite rapidly and soon became very worn and patchy. National marking and the codes were generally painted around but sometimes the *Gruppe/Geschwader* code was overpainted as were the black centres of the *balkenkreuze* and *hakenkreuze*. Following the spring thaw, the temporary paint was washed off, revealing the original permanent camouflage paint, but the same procedure was undertaken in the winters of 1942/1943 and 1943/1944.

National marking changes

Towards the end of 1943, new, simplified, national markings were being introduced on newly manufactured aircraft on the production line. Initially just the outer thin black border/trim was deleted, in all the *balkenkreuz* and *hakenkreuz* positions, forming a black centre with a white border – those above the wings having narrower borders than those on the fuselage sides and under the wings – but then, at the beginning of 1944, 'outline only' style markings started to appear on the wing upper surfaces and fuselage sides, where effectively the *balkenkreuze* were made up of four right angled 'arms' forming a cross shape and the *hakenkreuze* were merely outlines. On production line Ju 87s, the underwing *balkenkreuze* generally remained as the simplified black cross with broad white border style. Being 'open' markings, the underlying camouflage colours 'showed through' and occasionally the 'insides' of the crosses, especially those on the fuselage, were 'filled in' with a darker colour, such as RLM 70 *Schwarzgrün*.

Like the Stukas operating in Italy in 1943/44, later Ju 87D and G variants operating on the Eastern Front, especially those operating with the night harassment *Nachtschlachtgruppen*, often had the so-called *westenmüller* mirror-wave/meander scribble pattern applied over the top surfaces 'in the field' – this time in what appears to be light grey, possibly RLM 76 *Lichtblau*. As was the case with the Italian-based Stukas, the *westenmüller* was often applied over the national markings and sometimes the codes, again the *Gruppe/Geschwader* codes and often the last (*Staffel* i/d) letter, just leaving the individual aircraft letter untouched.

In late-1944, the letter/number-number/letter *Geschwader* or *Gruppe* code presentation on the fuselage sides of all Luftwaffe aircraft that carried these four-character codes including Ju 87s, was reduced to approximately 1/5th the size of the individual aircraft letter and *Staffel* code letter. This change almost coincided with the re-designation of all the Stuka units into dedicated *Schlachtgeschwader* (Ground Attack Groups).

Local tactical markings

The Luftwaffe used various tactical markings as a form of rapid identification as described earlier, throughout World War II. However, additional localised markings were also employed from time to

A Ju 87D-3, from II./*Sturzkampfgeschwader* 77, (or maybe *Schlachtgeschwader* 77 by this time?) judging by the codes – S2+NM – taxiing through the spring mud in early 1944 on a forward airfield on the Eastern Front, with its mainwheel undercarriage spats sensibly removed. As with Mediterranean and North African based Luftwaffe aircraft, the position of the yellow Eastern Front Theatre fuselage band varied which, in this instance, was just to the rear of the *balkenkreuz* causing part of the code to be painted over it. The Stuka in the background appears to be still in a weathered upper surface white winter finish.

A Ju 87D-3, originally operated by StG 3 judging by the 'diving crow' on the cowling side, photographed at Sidi Haneish (LG 13) in North Africa in November 1942 after being captured by British Commonwealth forces. It was painted yellow on its under surfaces and up the fuselage sides – the demarcation line can just be made out mid-way along the rear fuselage – and RAF markings applied by 601 Squadron, who were flying from the area at the time. The unit's code, 'UF', was also applied on the fuselage sides, in front of the roundels, (hidden by the wing in this photograph), and it is understood that the aircraft was flown by Squadron pilots from November 1942 until February 1943. Its ultimate fate is unknown.

time, the most striking perhaps being the large yellow rear-facing chevron applied from the leading edge above and below the port wing on many aircraft operating with *Luftflotte* 4 in Hungary between September 1944, and up to the end of hostilities in 1945. Aircraft so marked, including the Stukas, often had additional thin diagonal bars on the rudder.

Unit badges and emblems

In line with the traditional Teutonic heraldry of the German armed forces, the Luftwaffe made widespread use of unit badges and emblems, which were duly painted on the aircraft, in the case of the Ju 87, (all sub-types), invariably carried on forward fuselage just below the windscreen and could, and have, filled books in their own right. (q.v. *'Luftwaffe Emblems 1935-1945'* by Barry Ketley and Mark Rolfe, Flight Recorder Publications, 2012)

Foreign-operated Stukas

Junkers Ju 87s operated by 'foreign' air forces were invariably delivered in the standard RLM 70/71 'greens' upper surface splinter camouflage scheme, with RLM 65 blue/grey under surfaces. Those aircraft delivered directly off the production line from the manufacturer, would have had the Luftwaffe national markings deleted during the painting stage and the recipient countries' national markings applied. Aircraft delivered from existing Luftwaffe stocks, are noticeable in that the *balkenkreuze* and *hakenkreuze* were overpainted using RLM shades or paint from the recipient's stocks.

Regia Aeronautica

Italian *Regia Aeronautica* Stukas featured a white 'Savoy Cross', (from the House of Savoy's coat of arms), painted on the rudder and across on to the fin, with the fasci national insignia, black triple fascio on a white disc outlined in black, carried under the wings – no markings were carried above the wings. A white Mediterranean Theatre band was applied around the rear fuselage, and some Ju 87Bs and Rs operating in Libya in the summer of 1941 had the spinner and front section of the cowling painted yellow. Most of the Bs and Rs operating in the campaigns in Yugoslavia, Greece and Albania featured a yellow band around the mid cowling area, which extended on to and under the radiator housing.

As the *Regia Aeronautica* Stuka *Gruppi* (Wings) were operated as semi-autonomous units, generally, just the *Squadriglia* (squadron) number was applied to the rear fuselage, sometimes on the white band, sometimes in front of it and sometimes to the rear of it, or as in 237ª *Squadriglia's* case for example, on the outer faces of the mainwheel fairing, in either red or white. Individual aircraft identification numbers were applied, either on the fuselage, or on the mainwheel fairing, in black, white or red, the relevant *Squadriglia* colours, the 216ª having red roman, (instead of arabic), numerals, on the white fuselage band. In the 239ª *Squadriglia's* case the propeller spinner tips were also painted red. Unit badges, such as 237ª *Squadriglia's* bomb-riding devil or 239ª *Squadriglia's* dive-bombing goose, were applied to the fuselage or the mainwheel fairings. An Italian

Top: A pair of Ju 87Bs from 208ª *Squadriglia*, 101° *Gruppo, Regia Aeronautica* photographed on operations along the Greco-Albanian border in November 1940. Finished in the standard Luftwaffe RLM 70/71/65 scheme with the German national markings painted out, Italian Stukas featured a white 'Savoy Cross', (from the House of Savoy's coat of arms), painted on the rudder/fin, with the fasci national insignia, black triple fascio on a white disc outlined in black, under the wings. No markings were carried above the wings. A white Mediterranean Theatre band was applied around the rear fuselage and some Ju 87Bs and Rs operating in the campaigns in Yugoslavia, Greece and Albania had a yellow band painted around the mid cowling area, as illustrated by these two *Picchiatelli*. The nickname, given to the Stuka by *Regia Aeronautica* aircrew, was derived from *picchiatello* – meaning 'crazy' – but it was also the name of an Italian cartoon character, the 'Little Woodpecker', and is also the diminutive form of the verb *picchiare*, 'to dive';, the result, in effect, means 'crazy dive bomber'!)

military serial often replaced the German work number in white at the fin top.

No Ju 87Bs or Rs appear to have made it to the Armistice of September 1943, and the few Ju 87Ds that were left to serve in the Italian Co-Belligerent Air Force *(Aviazione Cobelligerante Italiana,* ACI), which was formed in southern Italy in October 1943 and formed the basis of the post-war *Aeronautica Militare Italiana* (AMI, Italian Air Force), appear to have been relegated to the training role after a few bombing missions in the Balkans, indeed the ACI never operated over Italian territory, to avoid any possible encounter between Italian-manned aircraft fighting on opposite sides. The *Regia Aeronautica* national markings were painted over, including the white fuselage band and unit markings, and green/white/red roundels were applied to the fuselage sides and above and below the wings.

A small section of the *Regia Aeronautica* remained under German control in the north, and was renamed as the National Republican Air Force (*Aeronautica Nazionale Repubblicana*, or ANR), but it is doubtful if any Ju 87s were used operationally by the ANR.

Hungary

The first ex-Luftwaffe Ju 87Bs that were transferred to the *Magyar Királyi Honvéd Légierő* (MKHL – Royal Hungarian Air Force) were allocated to the 2/2 *Zuhanobombazo szazad* (2nd Dive Bomber Squadron). Although most appear to have retained their ex-Luftwaffe RLM 70/71 upper surface 'splinter' scheme, photos of some Hungarian 'Bertas' show a wavy three-tone scheme, possibly in the Hungarian Stone Grey, Earth Brown, and Dark Green shades which may have been applied over the RLM scheme, or maybe this was simply just areas of a light brown/tan applied over the RLM 70/71. The Ju 87As that arrived in March 1942 for training duties were similarly camouflaged. Later, deliveries of Ju 87D-3s and D-5s that arrived during the spring of 1943, some of which were also allocated to 102/1 *Zuhanobombazo szazad* appear to have retained the RLM 70/71/65 scheme throughout their service, but all the Stukas had yellow Eastern Front Theatre fuselage bands and wing tip under surfaces.

The overt emergence of the MKHL in 1938 led to the re-introduction of the red/white/green triangle/chevron insignia originally used in 1919, applied facing in the direction of flight, from the trailing to leading edge, on both surfaces of the wing and across the fin and rudder. Then, in late 1941/early 1942, a revised national marking was introduced, comprising a black square with a superimposed white cross, applied to both surfaces of the wings and the fuselage sides. The red/white/green Hungarian national colours were retained on the tail surfaces, but in broad bands across the fin and rudder and both surfaces of the tailplanes. From early 1944, many aircraft, including the Ju 87s reduced the size and area of the tail markings, restricting the tri-colour bands to just the top of the rudder and the tips of the tailplanes. The white cross was also sometimes painted over in grey to reduce visibility.

The four character *Magyar Királyi Honvéd Légierő* coding system was prefixed by a letter – B in the case of bombers which included the Ju 87 – followed by three numbers, positioned on the fuselage sides. Prior to the introduction of the black square/white cross marking, the full code was applied with the letter separated from the numbers by a dot, but when the black square/white cross marking was introduced the letter and first number, still separated by a dot, was applied to the left of the fuselage marking and the remaining numbers to the right – e.g. B.7+03.

Romania

The *Forţele Aeriene Regale ale României* (Royal Romanian Air Force, FARR), operated over forty Ju 87Ds from the summer of 1943 until early 1945, equipping *Grupul 3° Bombardement Picaj* (No 3 Bomber Group), made up of *Escadrilas* (squadrons) 73, 81 and 85. Coming from ex-Luftwaffe stocks, they remained in the RLM 70/71/65 scheme and had the *balkenkreuze* and *hakenkreuze* overpainted and the new Romanian national markings, introduced in May 1941, consisting of a yellow cross, (Michael the Brave Cross), outlined in blue with a red/yellow/blue roundel in the centre, which was carried on the fuselage sides and below the wings, but for some reason, not above the wings. Also, Romanian Stukas did not have the blue/yellow/red rudder stripes applied at this time.

Following the coup (inspired by King Michael) on 23 August 1944, Romania accepted an Allied armistice offer and ceased all military action against Allied forces and joined the war against Germany. To reflect this change of sides, the Michael's Cross marking was overpainted, and the pre-war style red-yellow-blue roundel re-introduced, positioned on the fuselage and wings (albeit, once again, only on the wing undersides on Ju 87s). The tricolour rudder stripes were retained, and applied at the top 1/3 of the rudder on Romanian Ju 87Ds.

Individual aircraft numbers were applied, in white, on the rudder, and later, after the application of rudder stripes, on the fin, with names such as *'Hai Pusa'* (Come on Pusha), *'Måt'* (pussy cat) and *'Frt. Illuta'* (in memory of *Fruntas* (Private First Class) Illuta) written in white on the cowling sides.

Croatia

The handful of Ju 87Rs (thought to be around six) that served with 3 (Croat)./KGr 1, a mixed German-Croat unit, as part of the *Hrvatska Zrakoplovna Legija*, (Croatian Air Force Legion, or *Kroatische Luftwaffen Legion* in German), operated in the Balkans during 1944. All the 'Richards' appear to have been finished in the standard RLM 70/71/65 scheme, but with the Luftwaffe markings overpainted and a modified version of a *balkenkreuz* with the lower vertical arm reduced in width and curved to the left, applied to the fuselage sides – and possibly above and below the wings.

The Coat of Arms of the fascist State of Croatia (*Nezavisna Država Hrvatska*, NDH) a German puppet state established in parts of occupied Yugoslavia after the invasion by the Axis powers in April 1941 – comprising a shield with red and white checks, above which was the letter 'U' (for *Ustaše*, the fascist government) surrounded by a red stylised border – was carried under the windscreen of at least one of the unit's aircraft, coded 'white 2' on the rudder, which also had a yellow fuselage band forming the background to the fuselage cross.

Slovakia

In return for Slovakian military support on the Eastern Front, Germany gave the Slovak Air Force (*Slovenské Vzdušné Zbrane*, SVZ), a quantity of aircraft that included a number of Ju 87D-5s. These were assigned to the 11th *Letka* (Squadron) during 1943. Possibly delivered direct from the manufacturers – some sources state they were assembled in Slovakia with at least three being recorded with pre-war Czechoslovakian Civil Registrations (OK-XAA, OK-XAB and OK-XAC) on their fuselages. They were finished in the standard Luftwaffe RLM 70/71/65 scheme, but probably devoid of Luftwaffe markings. *Slovenské Vzdušné Zbrane* markings (a white bordered blue cross with a red disc in the centre) were applied to both surfaces of the wings and on either side of the fin. Eastern Front identification markings in the form of a yellow rear fuselage band and yellow areas under the wing tips were also applied. Codes, beginning with a 'B' then a number, starting from '1' were applied to the fuselage, in white, with the number repeated in miniature at the base of the rudder.

Bulgaria

Approximately twelve Ju 87Rs were supplied to the Bulgarians from ex-Luftwaffe stocks during the summer of 1943, but were probably not used on combat missions, being used as operational trainers instead. Later, some 30 plus (some references state as many as 50 plus) Ju 87D-3s and D-5s saw service with the Bulgarian Air Force, (*Vozdushni Voyska*), albeit briefly, on anti-partisan operations in Yugoslavia during the early summer of 1944.

All the Stukas would have originally been finished in the standard Luftwaffe RLM 70/71/65 scheme, with Luftwaffe markings painted out, and Bulgarian insignia applied. This had changed in 1941, from the red/white/yellow Medal of Bravery marking (a Maltese-style cross, with crossed swords and lion rampant in the centre) introduced in 1937, to the black saltire cross upon a white square, carried on both surfaces of the wings and on the fuselage sides. Yellow Eastern Front Theatre bands were applied in front of the Bulgarian saltire on the fuselage, and yellow wing tips on the under surfaces. When Bulgaria changed sides in September 1944, the yellow fuselage band and wingtips were painted white.

The Bulgarian Air Force, (*Vozdushni Voyska*), was made up of several Air Regiments (*Orljak*) each comprising a fighter, a bomber and two reconnaissance squadrons (*Yato*). The Ju 87Ds served with 1/2 *Orljak* (1st Air Regiment), 2nd *Shturmovi Yato* (Ground Attack Squadron). An individual aircraft identification number, in white, was applied to the rear fuselage. Recorded airframes include a Ju 87R coded 'white 8', Ju 87D-5 'white 24', Ju 87D-5 'white 30' which also had a white spinner with red spiral and red/green horizontal bands on the rudder, and Ju 87D-5 'white 46' which had a red spinner. 'White 46' also had its upper surfaces overpainted with the so-called *westenmüller* mirror-wave/meander scribble pattern, applied over the RLM 70/71, 'in the field', in what appears to be light grey, possibly RLM 76 *Lichtblau*.

Opposite page, lower: As the *Regia Aeronautica* Stuka *Gruppi* (Wings) were operated as semi-autonomous units, generally, just the *Squadriglia* (squadron) number was applied, invariably on the rear fuselage, sometimes on the white band, sometimes to the rear of it, or sometimes in front of it as in this case of a 209ª *Squadriglia* Ju 87R-2, (WNr 5763), which was captured by British Commonwealth forces in September 1941. This aircraft also had the spinner and whole front section of the cowling painted yellow which was a feature of Ju 87Bs and Rs operating in Libya in the summer of 1941. The aircraft also displays its individual aircraft identity in the form of a white numeral (18) on the outer face of the mainwheel fairing. Curiously, the black triple fascio on the white disc under the wings has been applied facing backwards. *Author's collection*

Junkers Ju 87V4, WNr 4924, D-UBIP, Rechlin-Lärz, Germany, 1936 | D-UBIP was one of the early prototypes for the Ju 87A-0 series and was left in an unpainted natural metal finish, with just the civil registration letters on the fuselage and above the wings. A black swastika on a white disc over a broad red band was applied across the fin and rudder, with just a strip at the fin leading edge left in bare natural metal. The aircraft's *werknummer (WNr)* was applied in small black characters on the tailplane tips. Rechlin-Lärz airfield, near Mecklenburg, Western Pomerania, Germany, was the Luftwaffe's main testing ground, (*Erprobungsstelle*) for new aircraft designs.

Junkers Ju 87A-0, 29•4, of *Versuchsjagdstaffel* 88, based at Calamocha, Spain, March 1938 | In January 1938, three production Ju 87A-0s were sent to Spain, and were allocated to VJ/88, the Legion's Experimental Fighter *Staffel*. The aircraft were finished in the three-tone RLM 61/62/63 upper surface 'splinter/segmented' camouflage scheme with *Hellblau* 65 under surfaces, introduced at the end of 1936. Like most of the other Condor Legion aircraft, the Ju 87As sported a white rudder with a black saltire cross with black discs with white diagonal saltires above and below the wings, and white wingtips. The unit's badge, an umbrella and a bowler hat within a white diamond, (a play on the crew's pseudo-civilian status), was painted on the outer face of the port undercarriage fairing, however, this was deemed inappropriate by higher authority and was replaced by a 'Jolanthe the Pig' cartoon – see the Condor Legion Ju 87B, illustration.

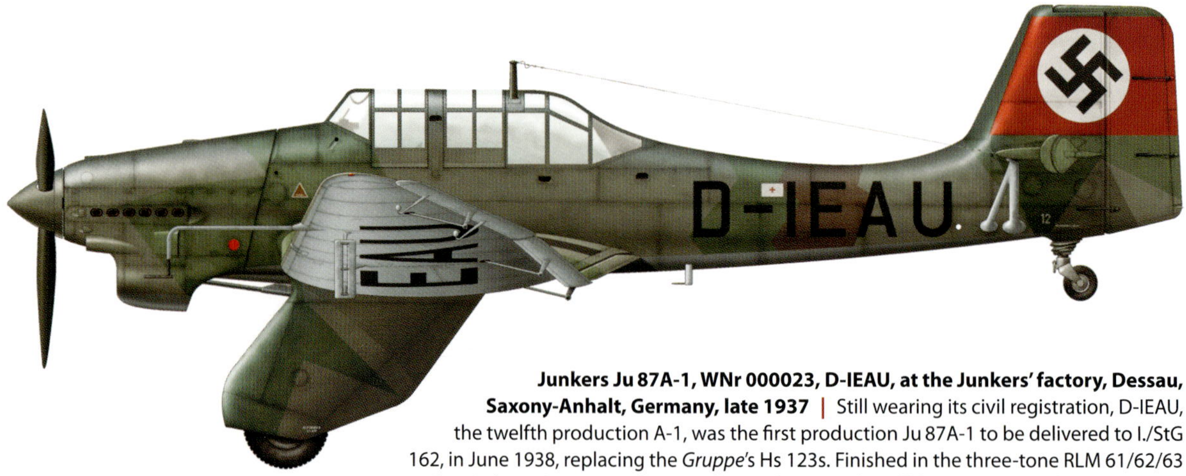

Junkers Ju 87A-1, WNr 000023, D-IEAU, at the Junkers' factory, Dessau, Saxony-Anhalt, Germany, late 1937 | Still wearing its civil registration, D-IEAU, the twelfth production A-1, was the first production Ju 87A-1 to be delivered to I./StG 162, in June 1938, replacing the *Gruppe*'s Hs 123s. Finished in the three-tone RLM 61/62/63 upper surface 'splinter/segmented' camouflage scheme with *Hellblau* 65 undersurfaces, the black civil registration letters were carried above and below the wings and on the fuselage sides. The fin and rudder had the black swastika on a white disc over a broad red band, which it retained when serving with StG 162.

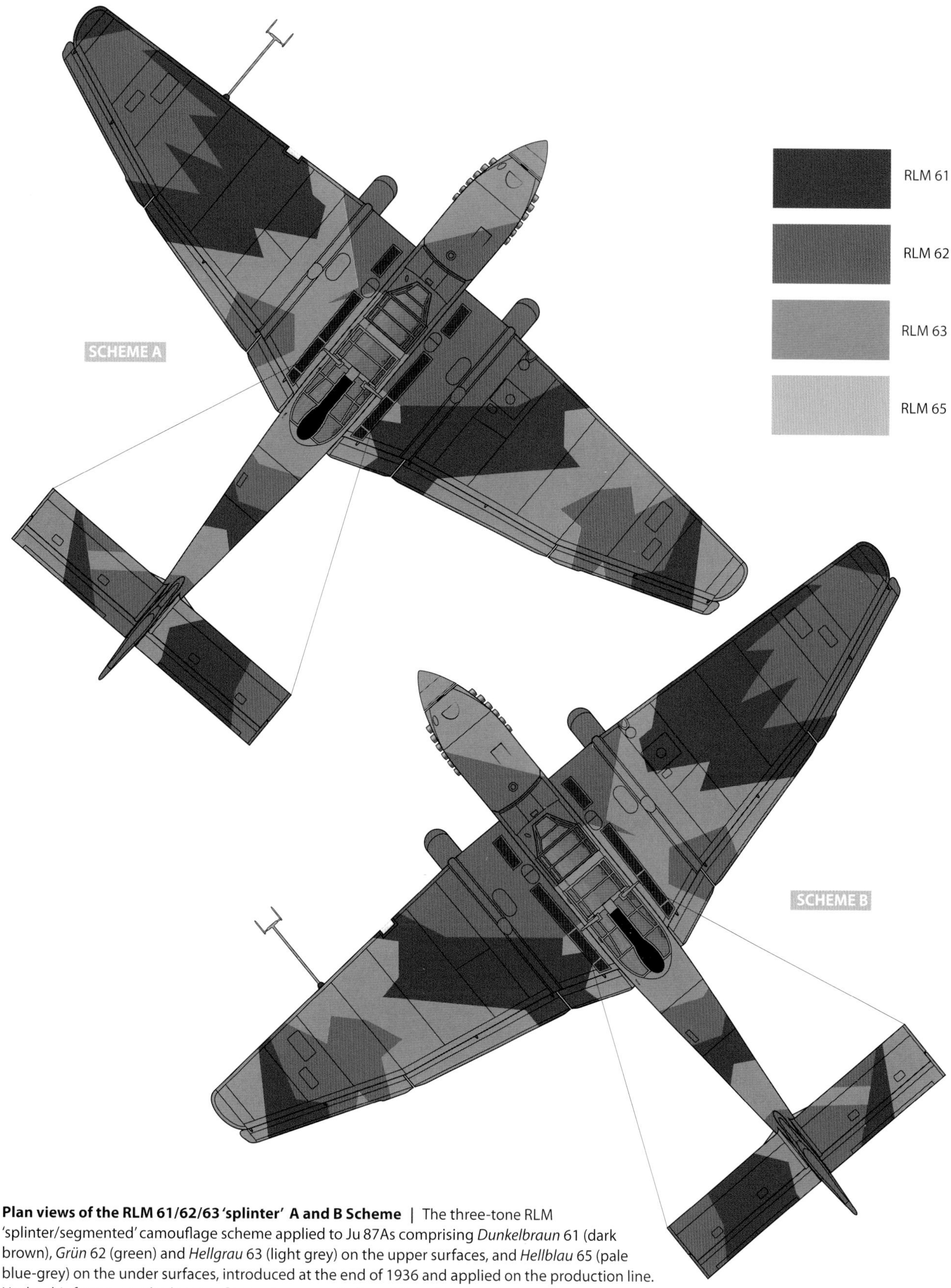

Plan views of the RLM 61/62/63 'splinter' A and B Scheme | The three-tone RLM 'splinter/segmented' camouflage scheme applied to Ju 87As comprising *Dunkelbraun* 61 (dark brown), *Grün* 62 (green) and *Hellgrau* 63 (light grey) on the upper surfaces, and *Hellblau* 65 (pale blue-grey) on the under surfaces, introduced at the end of 1936 and applied on the production line. Under this factory-applied camouflage scheme, each aircraft type (from each aircraft manufacturer) had a different pattern (*Farben Sichtschutz*) for the sharp-edged 'splinter/segment' design, laid out on a grid pattern on factory camouflage paint drawings, and while a specific 'splinter/segment' design was used for each manufacturers' individual aircraft type, they were produced in two basic patterns, which were mirror images of each other, known as Scheme A and Scheme B, (*Sichtschutzschema* A and B) as illustrated here.

Further, the RLM 61, 62 and 63 upper surface camouflage colours used in the Scheme A and the Scheme B patterns, could be, and were, often transposed, amongst the aircraft in a production batch, effectively giving up to six camouflage variations that could be applied to a particular aircraft type.

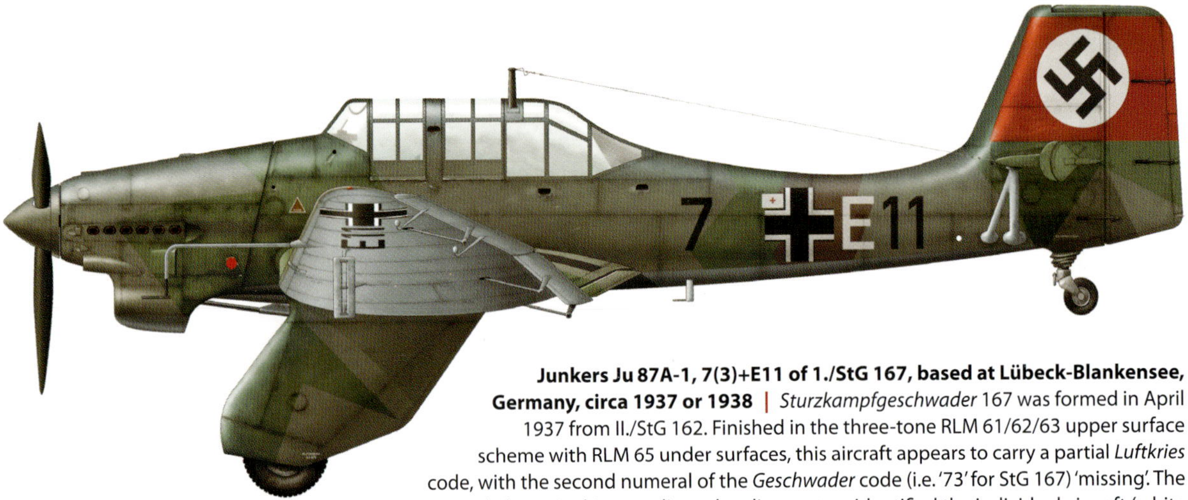

Junkers Ju 87A-1, 7(3)+E11 of 1./StG 167, based at Lübeck-Blankensee, Germany, circa 1937 or 1938 | *Sturzkampfgeschwader* 167 was formed in April 1937 from II./StG 162. Finished in the three-tone RLM 61/62/63 upper surface scheme with RLM 65 under surfaces, this aircraft appears to carry a partial *Luftkries* code, with the second numeral of the *Geschwader* code (i.e. '73' for StG 167) 'missing'. The other numerals/letter in this complicated coding system identified the individual aircraft (white 'E'), the *Gruppe* ('1' = I *Gruppe*) and the *staffel* ('1' = 1 *Staffel*). On 1 April 1938, I./StG 167 was redesignated as I./StG 168 and adopted the identification code '81', so it is possible that this particular machine was in the process of having its i/d codes changed. The black swastika on a white disc over a broad red band was applied across the fin and rudder, with just a strip at the fin leading edge left in camouflage.

Junkers Ju 87A-1, WNr 0029, S13+S29, of *Ergänzungs-Stukagruppe*, based at Jessau, East Prussia, circa August 1940 | *Ergänzungs-Stukagruppe* was formed in August 1940, equipped with Ju 87As to train fledgling Stuka pilots. Still camouflaged in the pre-war, three-tone RLM 61/62/63 upper surfaces with RLM 65 under surfaces scheme, it carried the coding system introduced in the mid-late 1930s for training unit machines, where the codes were prefixed with an 'S' (for *Schule*). In this instance, it is thought that the codes S13+S29 originally identified this Ju 87A-1 as being from *Luftkries* 1 (1), third unit (3), S Flight, aircraft '29'. *Ergänzungs-Stukagruppe* disbanded in August 1941, when based at Würzburg, becoming the *Ergänzungs Staffel* of StG 3. The white disc and broad red band of the fin and rudder marking had been painted out in camouflage colours, just leaving the black swastika, with a thin white outline.

Junkers Ju 87A-2, NG+RH, '40' of I./*Sturzkampfflieger-Schule* 2, based at Graz-Thalerhof, Austria, summer 1941 | From the summer of 1938 the Ju 87A had started to be phased out from frontline units in favour of the much improved 'Berta', however the 'Anton' still had a useful role to play as a trainer before finally being withdrawn in 1943-44. This example, carrying the *stammkennzeichen* (factory codes) NG+RH on the fuselage sides and under the wings, was operated by I./*Sturzkampfflieger-schule* 2, from the beginning of 1940, but still retained its pre-war RLM 61/62/63/65 scheme well in to 1941. Again, the original white disc and broad red band on the fin and rudder had been painted out in camouflage colours, just leaving the black swastika with a thin white outline. A white individual aircraft number, '40' was carried on the outer face of the undercarriage spats.

Junkers Ju 87B-1, 35+J26, of II./StG 163, based at Breslau-Schöngarten, Germany, early 1938 | Originally equipped with Henschel Hs 123As, over the winter of 1938/1939, II./*Sturzkampfgeschwader* 163 was one of the first units to re-quip with brand new Ju 87B-1s, while based at Breslau-Schöngarten. Finished in the then new two-tone green RLM 70/71 upper surface 'splinter' scheme with RLM 65 undersides, the aircraft carried the *Luftkries* code, with '35' identifying the *Geschwader* (StG 163), the red 'J' outlined in white being the individual aircraft letter, with the numeral '2', identifying II *Gruppe* and the numeral '6', the *Staffel* (i.e. 6 *Staffel*). On 1 May 1939, II./StG 163 was re-designated III./StG 2. The small narrow *balkenkreuze* were applied in all six positions and the *hakenkreuze* were positioned across the fin and rudder.

Junkers Ju 87B-1, 29•8, operated by 5 *Staffel Kampfgruppe* 88, aka the *Jolanthe Kette*, Condor Legion, early 1939 | Initially, three Ju 87B-1s were sent to Spain, in early January 1939, followed a few weeks later, by a further two or three, and joined 5.K/88. All were finished in the then new two-tone RLM 70/71 green upper surface 'splinter' scheme, and like the 'Antons', had Nationalist markings applied, with the codes carried on the fuselage sides. The unit's 'Jolanthe the Pig' badge (which replaced the previous umbrella and a bowler hat badge) was only applied on the port undercarriage spat. All the B-1s were returned to Germany during April 1939.

Junkers Ju 87B-1, S2+AC '10' of *Stab* II./StG 77, based at Breslau-Schöngarten, Germany, May 1939, flown by Major Alfons Orthofer, II *Gruppe Kommandeur* | II./StG 77 was formed in May 1939 at Breslau-Schöngarten from II./StG 165. S2+AC, the *Gruppenkommandeur*'s aircraft, had a striking red and white sharkmouth design, including eyes and nostrils, applied for publicity purposes when the German propaganda magazine '*Signal*' ran a special feature on the unit. Finished in the standard RLM 70/71/65 scheme with the then new broader-bordered fuselage and underwing crosses, S2+AC's sharkmouth was removed shortly afterwards. The spinner tip was in the *Stab* RLM 25 *Hellgrün* (green) with the individual aircraft letter in black with a green outline. The individual aircraft number '10' on the outer faces of both wheel spats was in white, with the individual aircraft letter 'A' repeated under the wing tips in black.

Junkers Ju 87B-1, A5+AB, of *Stab* I./StG.1, based at Jüterbog, Germany, summer 1939 | Immediately prior to the invasion of Poland, A5+AB, was the I *Gruppe Kommandeur's* machine, Major Werner Rentsch. Finished in the RLM 70/71/65 scheme, with narrow bordered crosses and centrally placed swastika, the white fuselage band indicated a *Stab* machine. The 'Diving Raven' insignia of I./StG 1 was applied to the outer faces of the spats on A5+AB rather than the more usual position on the nose. Also of interest is that the first letter of the *Geschwader* code has been applied at a lower level than the rest and although the individual aircraft letter should be in green as befits a *Gruppenstab* machine, it has been applied in white. The clear perspex access panel covering the emergency first aid kit on the fuselage side near the cross, remains unpainted which was a feature of early Ju 87B-1s.

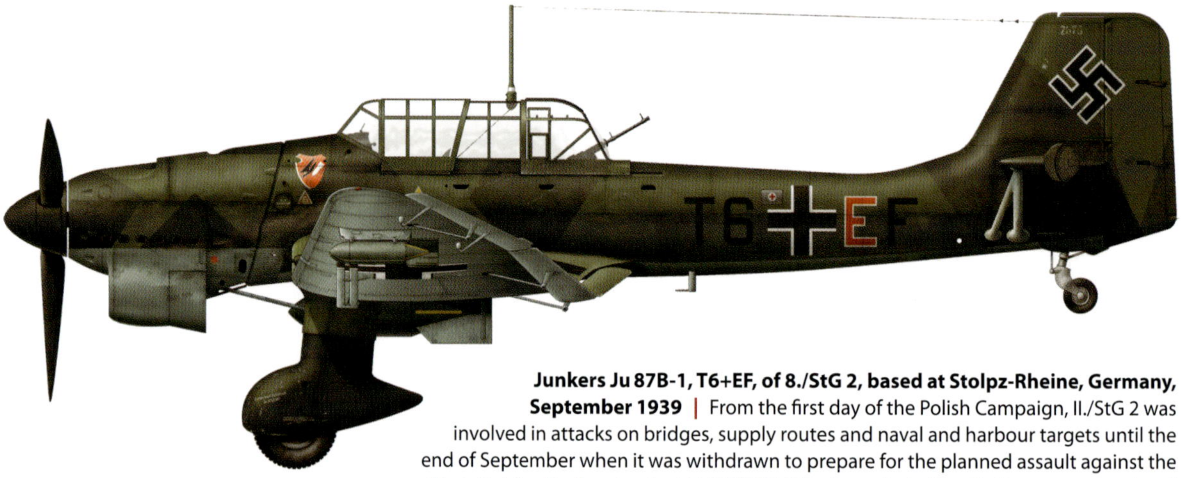

Junkers Ju 87B-1, T6+EF, of 8./StG 2, based at Stolpz-Rheine, Germany, September 1939 | From the first day of the Polish Campaign, II./StG 2 was involved in attacks on bridges, supply routes and naval and harbour targets until the end of September when it was withdrawn to prepare for the planned assault against the West. Finished in the standard RLM 70/71/65 scheme but still with the narrow-bordered *balkenkreuze*, although those under the wings were of much larger proportions. The aircraft carried the 8 *Staffel* badge, a black diving eagle outlined in white, carrying a white bomb in its claws, on a red stylised shield, on both sides of the nose and the 'last three' of the *werknummer* '329' were carried in white at the top of both sides of the fin. Of note is the high upper/under surface camouflage demarcation on the nose, a feature of many early Ju 87B-1s.

Junkers Ju 87B-1, 6G+AR, of 7./StG 51, based at various airfields in Belgium and France, during May/early June 1940 | It was in the Polish and French 'Blitzkrieg' campaigns that the fearful reputation of the 'Stuka' was established and III./StG 51, of which 7 *Staffel* was a component, was heavily committed in both. Operating initially from airfields in Belgium and then from France, during May 1940 and in to early June, the unit attacked ground targets before bombing evacuation shipping in the harbour and off the beaches of Dunkirk. Finished in the standard RLM 70/71/65 scheme, 6G+AR carried 7 *Staffel's* distinctive yellow eight-pointed star and black bull with comet trail emblem. Both the spinner ring and individual aircraft were in the *staffel* colour white.

Junkers Ju 87B-2, 6G+AD, of *Stab* III./StG 51, Cherbourg, France, June 1940 | Following the fall of France, III./StG 1 continued with anti-shipping operations, this time against coastal targets around the British Isles led by *Hauptmann* Anton Keil from mid-May until it was re-named II./StG 1 in July 1940. Finished in the standard RLM 70/71/65 scheme, there are two interesting points about this aircraft. The first concerns the light-coloured codes that all the *stabsschwarm* aircraft carried, which are shown here in RLM 25 *Hellgrün*, but it is possible that they were light blue, light grey or grey-green. The second concerns the unit badge which should be the silver 'Mailed Gauntlet on a yellow shield', but the reference photo used shows it to resemble a face, perhaps a personal marking and therefore a little artistic licence has been employed in the reproduction of this marking.

Junkers Ju 87B-2, L1+CU, of 10 *Staffel* IV.(Stuka)/LG 1, based at Tramecourt, France, August 1940 | *Lehrgeschwader* 1 (LG 1 – Operational Training Wing 1, whose various units originally formed during 1937 and 1938), was more of a multi-purpose Tactical Development unit, and operated Bf 109s, Bf 110s, Do 17s, He 111s, Ju 88s and Ju 87s within its four *Gruppen*. In the summer of 1940, IV *Gruppe*, comprised the *Gruppenstab*, plus 10, 11 and 12 *Staffeln*, and was equipped with Ju 87Bs, undertaking operations against the British Isles from bases at Tramecourt and Hesdin in the Pas-de-Calais. Finished in the standard RLM 70/71/65 scheme, the aircraft carried IV./(Stuka) LG 1's emblem, a pale blue shield with a devil holding a trident and riding a bomb, under the windscreen, which was 'handed' on both sides. Of note is the slightly higher positioning of the fuselage codes.

Junkers Ju 87B-2, J9+BL, of 9./StG 1, based at Ostend Belgium, late November 1940 | Following heavy losses in July and August, the Stuka was withdrawn from daylight operations, but returned over the British Isles with the start of the night 'Blitz' at the end of September. At first sight, J9+BL is a bit of an enigma, as although a 9 *Staffel* machine it has 3 *Staffel*'s i/d code 'L' and 6 *Staffel*'s 'torch-carrying devil riding a bomb' badge under the windscreen. However, the unit originally belonged to I./StG 186 which was re-designated III./StG 1 in July 1940 and continued to use the 'J9' code and its original *staffel* letters, H, K and L – but why it carried 6./StG 1's emblem is anybody's guess! Finished in the standard RLM 70/71/65 scheme, the undersides were overpainted with a temporary black wash for nocturnal operations, as were the codes and national insignia.

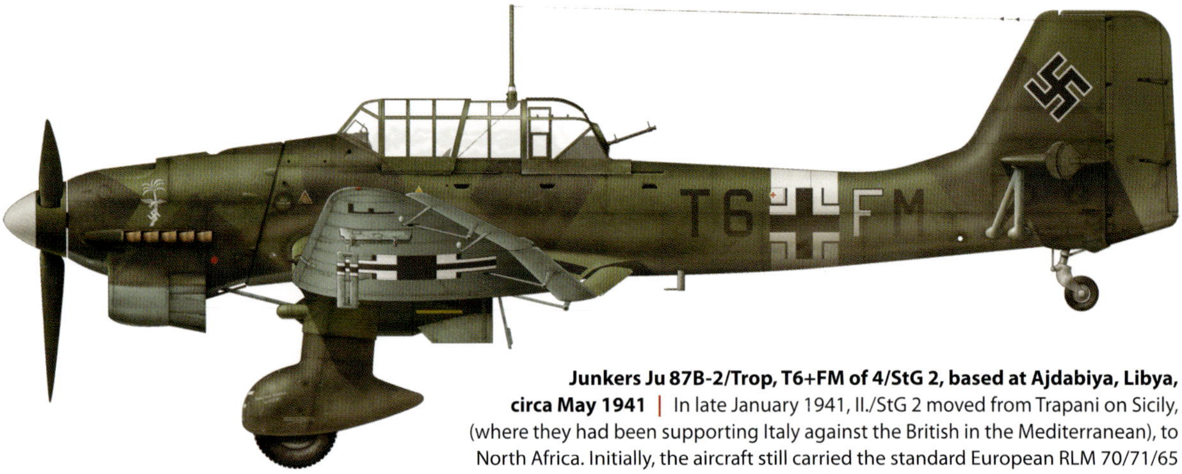

Junkers Ju 87B-2/Trop, T6+FM of 4/StG 2, based at Ajdabiya, Libya, circa May 1941 | In late January 1941, II./StG 2 moved from Trapani on Sicily, (where they had been supporting Italy against the British in the Mediterranean), to North Africa. Initially, the aircraft still carried the standard European RLM 70/71/65 scheme, with just white identification markings to reflect their theatre of operations. These i/d markings took several forms including a fuselage band, often as a 'background' to the *balkenkreuze* as illustrated on T6+FM. The spinner tip and the individual aircraft letter are also white, the latter with a dark (possibly black) outline, which was repeated on the front of both undercarriage spats in white. The *Deutsches Afrika Korps* symbol, a swastika and palm tree, was carried on the nose, in white.

Junkers Ju 87B-2/Trop, T6+DP, of 6./StG 2, based at Tmimi, Libya, circa autumn 1941, flown by Lt Hubert Polz | Flown by Lt Hubert Polz, one of the unit's most successful pilots, at some point during the summer of 1941 following the unit's move to North Africa after operations against Malta, a large 'snake' marking was applied to the fuselage of T6+DP (probably to both sides). The camouflage scheme was the standard RLM 70/71 'green' upper surfaces with bands and segments of what is thought have been Italian *Giallo Mimetico* (Camouflage Yellow) as the Luftwaffe didn't introduce the RLM desert colours of 79 *Sandgelb* and 80 *Olivgrün* until early 1942. The trailing edge of the rudder has also been overpainted in what appears to be RLM 65, but whether this was for damage repair or camouflage effect, (i.e. optically reducing the profile of the rudder), is unknown.

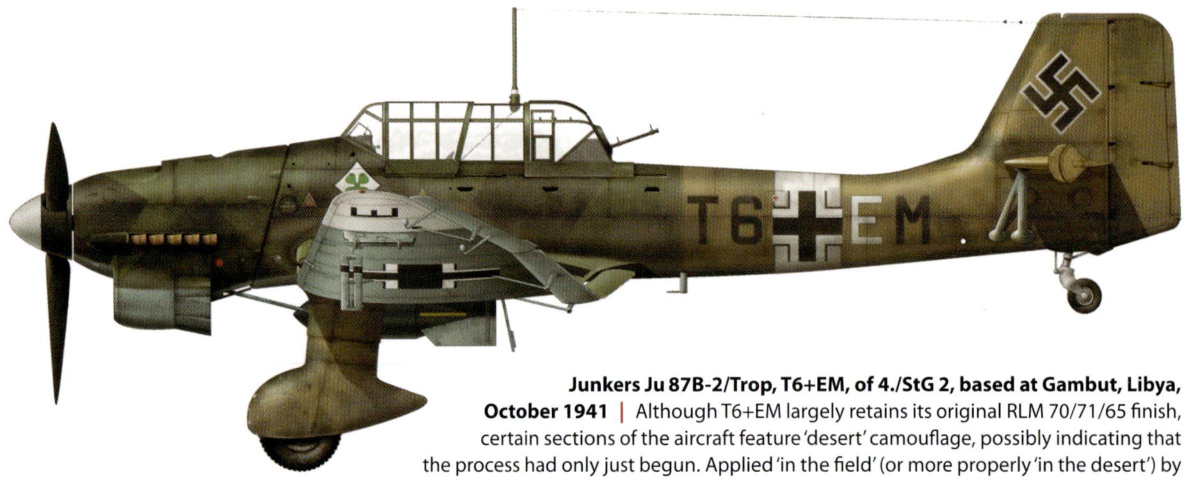

Junkers Ju 87B-2/Trop, T6+EM, of 4./StG 2, based at Gambut, Libya, October 1941 | Although T6+EM largely retains its original RLM 70/71/65 finish, certain sections of the aircraft feature 'desert' camouflage, possibly indicating that the process had only just begun. Applied 'in the field' (or more properly 'in the desert') by the groundcrew, the rear fuselage fin and rudder and undercarriage spats appear to have had a patchy application of a light tan shade, probably Italian *Giallo Mimetico*. A white fuselage band was applied 'behind' the *balkenkreuze*, plus white wing tip under surfaces. The white individual aircraft letter 'E', was repeated on the front of the undercarriage spats, and in black under the wing tips. The spinner tip was also in the *staffel* colour, white, and the emblem of 4./StG 2, a green four leaf clover on a white diamond edged in black was carried under the windscreen.

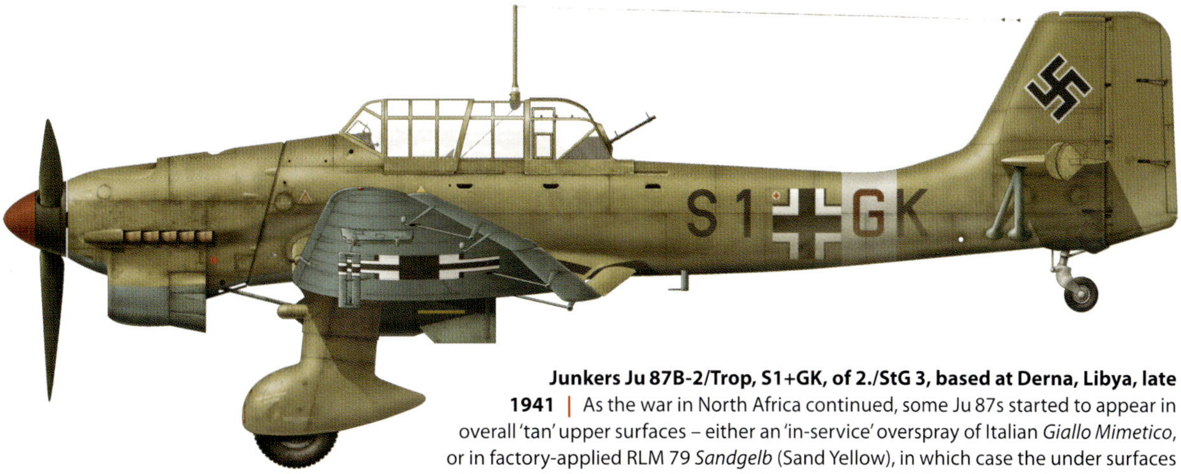

Junkers Ju 87B-2/Trop, S1+GK, of 2./StG 3, based at Derna, Libya, late 1941 | As the war in North Africa continued, some Ju 87s started to appear in overall 'tan' upper surfaces – either an 'in-service' overspray of Italian *Giallo Mimetico*, or in factory-applied RLM 79 *Sandgelb* (Sand Yellow), in which case the under surfaces would have been in the official Luftwaffe 'desert scheme' RLM 78 *Himmelblau* (Sky Blue) as illustrated on S1+GK. The white fuselage band was positioned aft of the fuselage cross, with the red individual aircraft letter 'G' applied over it on the port side, and the numeral '1' of the *Geschwader* code (S1) over it on the starboard side. No unit emblems appear to have been carried but the propeller spinner tip was in the *staffel* colour, red.

Junkers Ju 87R-2/Trop, S7+CA, of the *Geschwaderstab*/StG 3, based at Haggag-el-Quasaba, Egypt, late 1941 | This Ju 87R-2 was one of several 'Richards' on the strength of StG 3's *Geschwaderstab* while based at Haggag-el-Quasaba, near El Alamein, in September 1941. Finished in the standard RLM 70/71/65 scheme it had an intricate linear overspray of Italian *Giallo Mimetico* or maybe RLM 79 *Sandgelb*, to create a 'green mottle on a sand base' effect. The *Geschwaderstab* emblem, a white mosque and palm tree on sandy ground under a blue sky, was carried under the port windscreen, and on the starboard side cowling, just above the exhausts, is what appears to be I./StG 1's 'Diving Raven', indicating that the aircraft may have earlier served with that unit. No white fuselage band or white wingtips were applied, but the individual aircraft letter 'C' and the propeller spinner tip were in the *Geschwaderstab* blue.

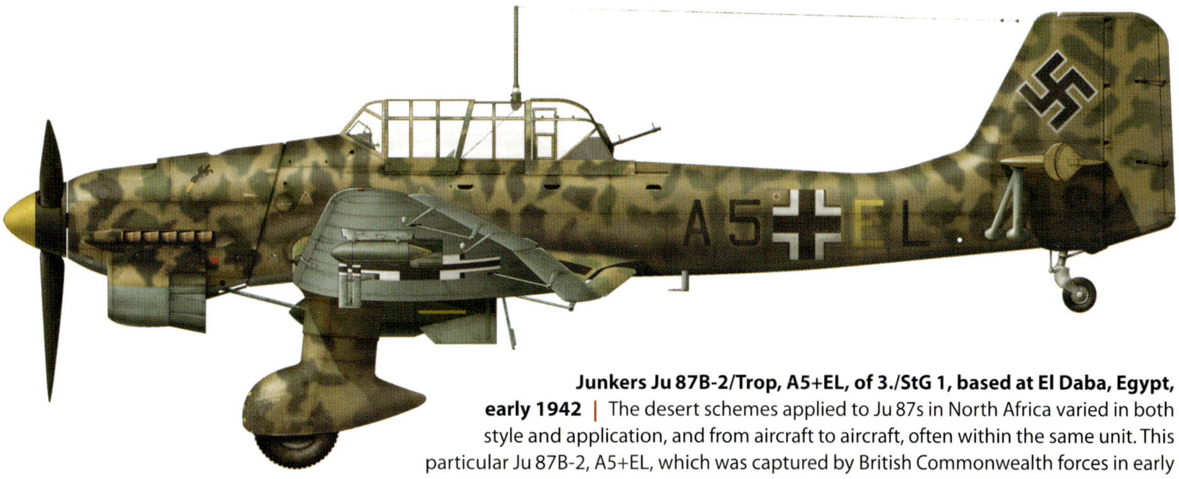

Junkers Ju 87B-2/Trop, A5+EL, of 3./StG 1, based at El Daba, Egypt, early 1942 | The desert schemes applied to Ju 87s in North Africa varied in both style and application, and from aircraft to aircraft, often within the same unit. This particular Ju 87B-2, A5+EL, which was captured by British Commonwealth forces in early 1942, is believed to have originally been finished in the standard RLM 70/71 upper surface scheme, but then had an overspray of RLM 79 *Sandgelb*, over which a mottle of RLM 80 *Olivgrün* was applied. The individual aircraft letter is in yellow, the *staffel* colour, as is the spinner tip, although the photograph used as reference shows the aircraft in a 'distressed' state and minus its rudder, engine cowling and spinner, so the camouflage on these areas has been estimated.

Junkers Ju 87R-2, A5+CH, of 1./StG 1, Krainici, Bulgaria, April 1941 | Temporarily transferred from operations against Malta, to take part in the invasion of Yugoslavia in April 1941, (prior to being sent to North Africa in June – see A5+EL on the previous page), I./StG 1's aircraft had high visibility yellow (RLM *Gelb* 04) markings applied to the nose cowlings and rudders like many other Luftwaffe aircraft involved in the Balkan Campaign. It would appear that no clear instructions regarding the extent of the areas to be painted yellow were issued, as in A5+CH's case the whole of the engine cowling and the whole tail section and both surfaces of the tailplanes, were painted yellow, as well as the wing tip under surfaces. I *Gruppe*'s 'Diving Raven' was carried on the cowling, carefully painted around when the yellow was applied, as too was the swastika on the fin.

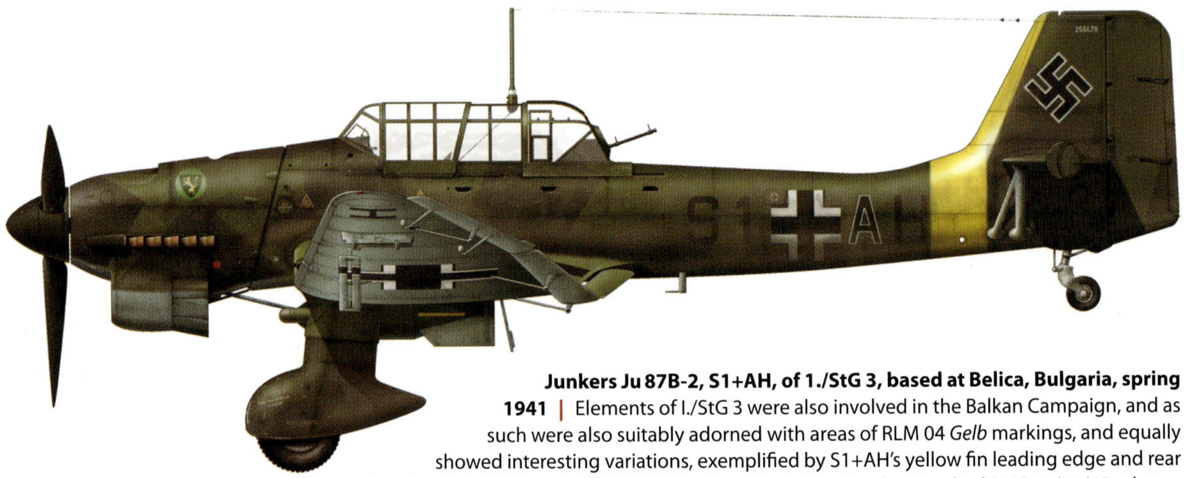

Junkers Ju 87B-2, S1+AH, of 1./StG 3, based at Belica, Bulgaria, spring 1941 | Elements of I./StG 3 were also involved in the Balkan Campaign, and as such were also suitably adorned with areas of RLM 04 *Gelb* markings, and equally showed interesting variations, exemplified by S1+AH's yellow fin leading edge and rear fuselage band. The rest of the 1 *Staffel* aircraft is finished in the standard RLM 70/71/65 scheme with black codes with just the individual aircraft letter 'A' being outlined in white. The unit badge of 1./StG 3, a yellow rampant griffon on dark green shield set within a lighter green disk, was carried on the nose. The propeller spinner was plain RLM 70 *Schwarzgrün*, without a coloured tip.

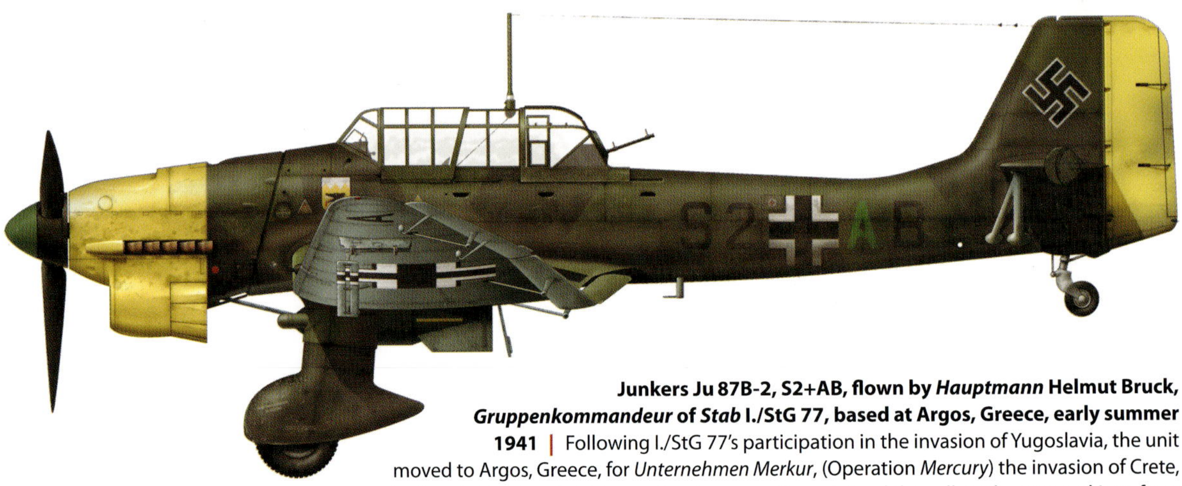

Junkers Ju 87B-2, S2+AB, flown by *Hauptmann* Helmut Bruck, *Gruppenkommandeur* of *Stab* I./StG 77, based at Argos, Greece, early summer 1941 | Following I./StG 77's participation in the invasion of Yugoslavia, the unit moved to Argos, Greece, for *Unternehmen Merkur*, (Operation *Mercury*) the invasion of Crete, in May 1941. Aircraft taking part in the operation retained the yellow theatre markings from their Balkan excursion, S2+AB having a yellow cowling front and yellow rudder. The rest of the aircraft was finished in the standard RLM 70/71/65 scheme with black codes, just the individual aircraft letter and tip to the propeller spinner being in the I *Gruppe Stab* colour of RLM 25 *Hellgrün*. *Stab* I./StG 77's emblem, a black wolf's head on a yellow shield with white segmented top, was carried on the nose.

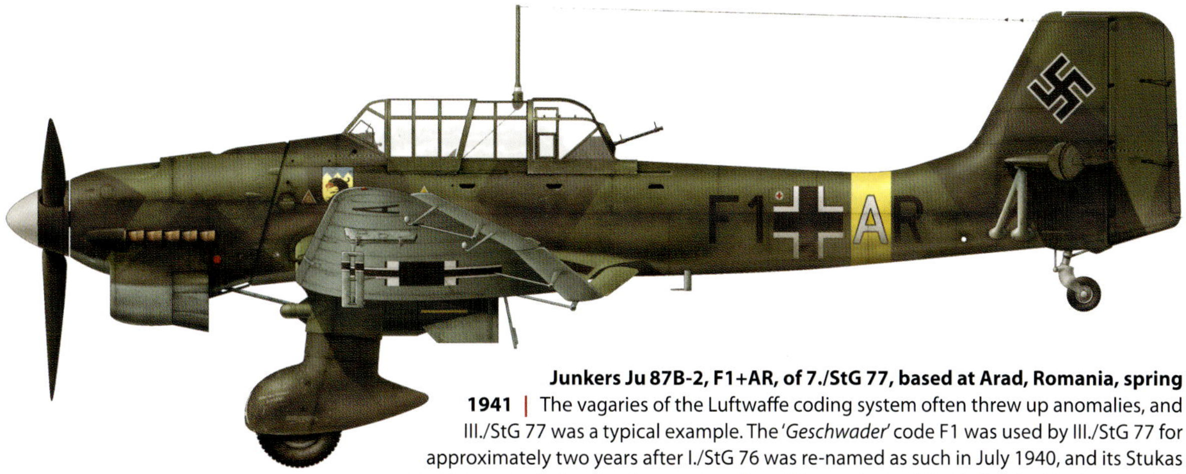

Junkers Ju 87B-2, F1+AR, of 7./StG 77, based at Arad, Romania, spring 1941 | The vagaries of the Luftwaffe coding system often threw up anomalies, and III./StG 77 was a typical example. The '*Geschwader*' code F1 was used by III./StG 77 for approximately two years after I./StG 76 was re-named as such in July 1940, and its Stukas carried this code during the German invasion of Greece in April 1941. Finished in the standard RLM 70/71/65 scheme, this particular aircraft merely carried a yellow Theatre band around the rear fuselage prompting the white individual aircraft letter 'A' to be outlined in black. The 7 *Staffel* badge, (used from 1941-43), a black eagle's head with red beak on a yellow shield with a blue segmented top, was carried under the windscreen, and the spinner tip was in white, with the individual letter repeated on the front of both undercarriage spats in white.

Plan view of the RLM 70/71 A Scheme 'splinter' pattern | Introduced in 1938, the new camouflage scheme was deemed to be more suitable for a continental European environment than the earlier RLM 61/62/63 combination. Comprising just two colours, both greens, RLM 70 *Schwarzgrün* (black green) and RLM 71 *Dunkelgrün* (dark green), again in a straight-edged 'splinter' pattern, it was applied using factory paint charts that were also based upon a grid. As with the RLM 61/62/63 scheme, it allowed the pattern to be mirrored, in A and B Schemes, and also have the two colours transposed, although it is doubtful whether the B Scheme was ever applied. The under surfaces remained in RLM 65 *Hellblau*.

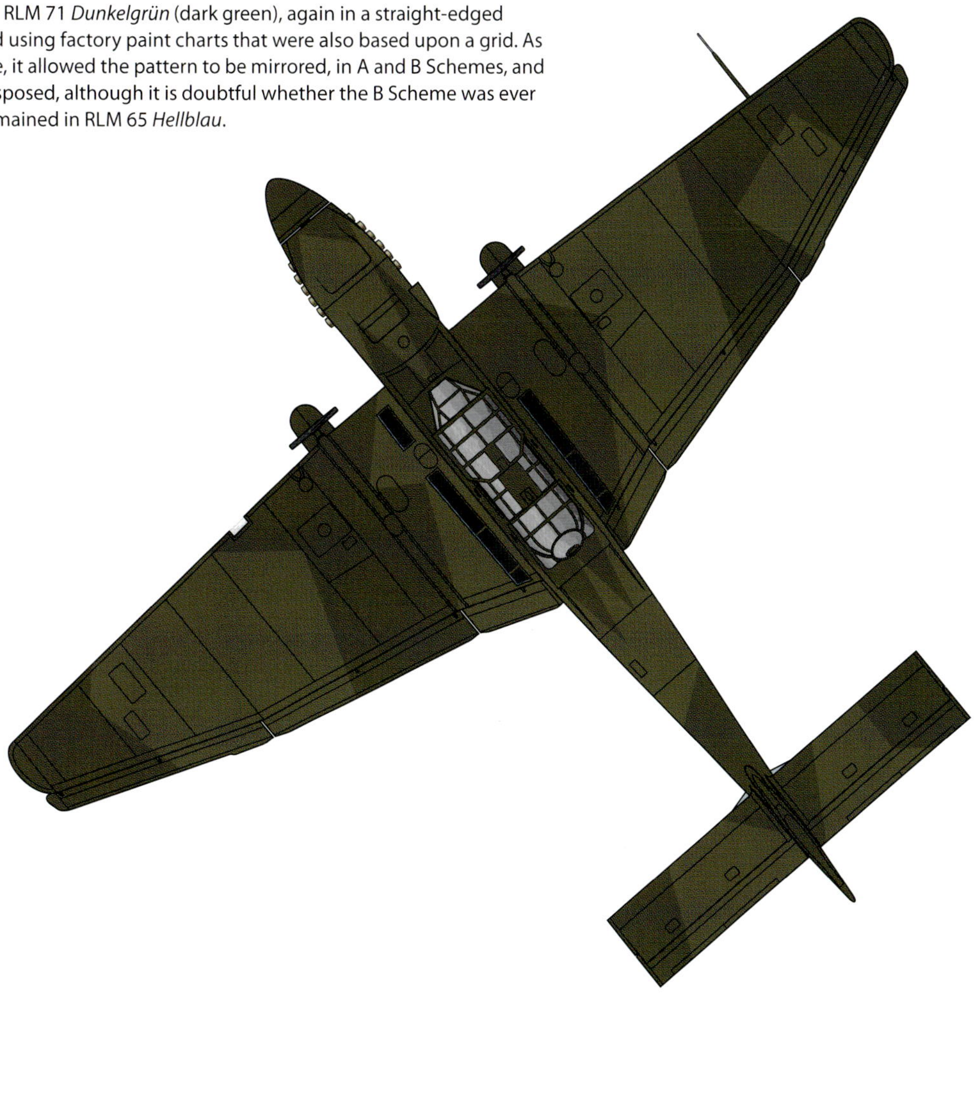

Junkers Ju 87B-2, S2+HM, of 4./StG 77, based around Orel, Russia, autumn 1941 | Operation *Barbarossa*, the invasion of the Soviet Union, commenced on 22 June 1941, and seven *Stukagruppen* were initially involved. As with Luftwaffe aircraft operating in the Balkan Campaign, additional identification markings were applied, and again yellow was chosen, this time in the form of a rear fuselage band. Finished in the standard RLM 70/71/65 scheme, S2+HM is illustrated in a weathered condition, the result of operating from rough forward airstrips. The propeller spinner tip and individual aircraft letter are both in the 4 *Staffel* colour – white: the latter on the fuselage sides with a thin black outline, and repeated just in white on the front of both undercarriage spats. The emblem of 4./StG 77, a black cockerel on a yellow shield with a red-segmented top, was carried under the windscreen. Also of note is the white-walled tailwheel tyre.

Junkers Ju 87B-2, T6+AD, *Stab* III./StG 2, based at Tyrkowo, Russia, late summer 1941 | Although T6+AD is often referred to as the aircraft flown by Hans-Ulrich Rudel, it was more likely the mount of *Hauptmann* Ernst-Siegfried Steen, or perhaps Major Gustav Pressler, who replaced Steen and commanded the *Gruppe* until May 1943. Finished in the standard RLM 70/71/65 scheme, the yellow fuselage band on T6+AD was placed forward of the fuselage cross in this instance and the aircraft had yellow wing tip undersurfaces. The propeller spinner tip was light blue as was the individual aircraft letter, repeated on the front of both undercarriage spats in white. The badge of III./StG 2, was based on the Slovak coat of arms, comprising a blue shield with a white double Byzantine cross standing on three red peaks. (Rudel became *Gruppenkommandeur* of III./StG 3, after being promoted to *Hauptmann*, in July 1943).

Junkers Ju 87B-2, 6G+AC, of *Stab* II./StG 1, based at Juchnow, about 150km south-west of Moscow, circa late 1941 | After the winter snows started to fall, the Luftwaffe gave many of its aircraft a coat of temporary white paint over the standard RLM 70/71 upper surface camouflage. This finish soon became very patchy, either as a result of hasty application or wear due to the extreme conditions experienced on the Eastern Front. National and unit markings were either painted around or masked off. The individual aircraft letter and propeller spinner tip on 6G+AC are in green (RLM 25 *Hellgrün*), with the under surfaces of the wing tips in yellow. Of note is the wider than usual yellow rear fuselage band. The *Stab* II./StG 1 emblem, a red eagle wearing a crown, with wings spread, on a white shield, (inherited from III./StG 51 in July 1940), was carried on the nose.

Junkers Ju 87D-1/Trop, S7+IR, of 7 *Staffel* III./StG 3, based at Derna, Libya, May/June 1942 | Amongst the first deliveries of the improved Ju 87D-1 sent to the Mediterranean and North Africa at the beginning of 1942, were a few examples finished in an 'desert' scheme applied on the manufacturer's production line, comprising RLM 79 *Sandgelb* upper surfaces with RLM 78 *Hellblau* under surfaces. Also, due to initial problems with the re-designed landing gear forks, many initial production D-1s were completed with the legs and spats from the Ju 87B-2, as illustrated by S7+IR. No unit badges appear to have been applied, but the individual aircraft and *staffel* letters (I and R) are both in white, (thinly outlined in black), which may have been a III./StG 3 affectation, as S7+KR's last two letters were both in the *staffel* colour red – (see below). The propeller spinner tip was also white, the *Staffel* colour.

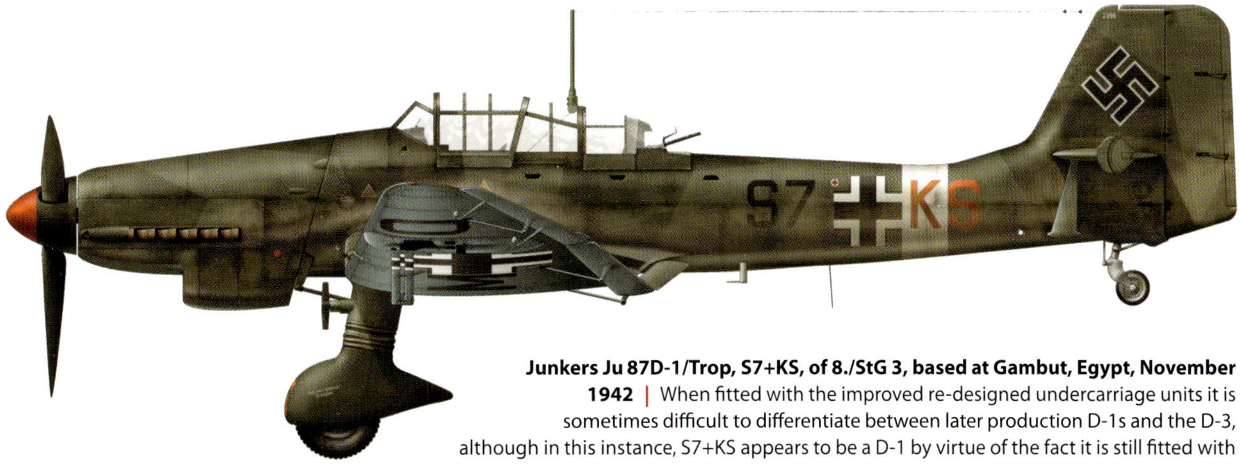

Junkers Ju 87D-1/Trop, S7+KS, of 8./StG 3, based at Gambut, Egypt, November 1942 | When fitted with the improved re-designed undercarriage units it is sometimes difficult to differentiate between later production D-1s and the D-3, although in this instance, S7+KS appears to be a D-1 by virtue of the fact it is still fitted with 'siren' mountings on the undercarriage legs. Finished in the standard RLM 70/71/65 scheme, with no attempt at any 'desert' colouring, what is again interesting is that the individual and the *staffel* letters (K and S) are both in the *staffel* colour, red, as is the tip of the propeller spinner. This particular aircraft, *werknummer* 2396, (applied in white at the top of the fin), was shot down on 1 November 1942. Both crew members – *Uffz* Otto Eckhardt and *Uffz* Herbery Wagner – were captured, albeit wounded.

Junkers Ju 87D-3/Trop, S7+AA, of *Geschwaderstab* StG 3, based at Haggag-el-Quasaba, Egypt, late 1942 | The Ju 87D-1 was quickly followed by the D-3, which incorporated extra armour for the engine and the cockpit area, which had the adverse effect of increased weight, so to help compensate, the D-3 was the first Stuka variant to be built without 'sirens' fitted to the undercarriage legs. This particular D-3 was flown by the *Geschwader Kommodore*, *Oberstleutnant* Walter Sigel, and was finished in the standard two-tone green RLM 70/71 upper surfaces with RLM 65 undersides, but then had patches of RLM 79 *Sandgelb*, (or maybe Italian *Giallo Mimetico*), on the fuselage sides and above the wings. The individual aircraft letter and the propeller spinner tip were in *Geschwaderstab* blue. The profile is illustrated carrying a 1,000kg SC1000 bomb under the centre section.

Junkers Ju 87D-1, J9+MH, of 7 *Staffel* III./StG 1, based at Orel, Russia, February 1943 | Some of the first Ju 87D-1s were also sent to the Eastern Front, and like those sent to the Mediterranean and North Africa, some were fitted with Ju 87B-style main undercarriage legs, like J9+MH illustrated here. Receiving its 'Doras' during January 1943, III./StG 1 immediately covered the standard RLM 70/71 upper surfaces with a coat of temporary white paint to blend in with the winter snows. Carrying the 'old' J9 codes and ex-StG 186 winged helmet and anchor badge on the cowling side, yellow Eastern Front rear fuselage band and wing tip under surfaces were applied. The individual aircraft letter 'M' in the *staffel* colour white, had a thin black outline, which was repeated on the front of the spats and the tip of the propeller spinner was quartered in black and white.

Junkers Ju 87D-3, S2+NM, of 4./StG 77, based in the Eastern Ukraine area, spring 1943 | During the spring thaws, the landing grounds became very muddy and it became expedient to remove the spats, as illustrated by this example, from 4./StG 77. Finished in the standard RLM 70/71/65 finish, all the temporary white paint has either been removed or, if a brand-new replacement, had never been applied at all. It is also very heavily exhaust stained, extending along the fuselage side and over the codes and the cross. The individual aircraft letter appears to be plain white, albeit stained, and the spinner tip is white. The Eastern Front fuselage band and wingtip undersides were yellow, and the 4./StG 77 badge, a black crowing cockerel on a yellow shield with red segmented top, was carried on the cowling side.

Junkers Ju 87D-5, Q9+MH, of 1./StG 5, based at Nautsi, near Kirkenes, Norway, summer 1944 | Reformed and re-equipped with Ju 87D-5s in June 1943, I./StG 5 was assigned to north-eastern Norway for operations over northern Finland. Finished in the standard RLM 70/71/65 scheme, with a yellow Eastern Front band around the rear fuselage and yellow wing tip undersurfaces, the national markings were the later 'open' white outline style, with the fuselage cross possibly having a dark grey centre. The *Geschwader* code (Q9) on the fuselage sides was the reduced, 1/5th, style, with the full-size individual aircraft letter 'M' in white, as was the extreme spinner tip. Of note are the two narrow white angled lines on the rudder, a common marking for aircraft serving in this area. Again, the main undercarriage spats have been removed and there is very heavy exhaust staining extending all along the fuselage side.

Ju 87D-8, E8+CH of 1./NSGr 9, northern Italy, summer 1944 | 1./*Nachtschlachtgruppe* 9 was originally formed in December 1943, but didn't receive Ju 87Ds until the spring of 1944. Operating from various landing grounds in northern Italy the aircraft were finished in the standard RLM 70/71/65 scheme overpainted with the so-called *westenmüller*/scribble pattern applied over the upper surfaces, 'in the field', sometimes in light tans such as *Giallo Mimetico* or RLM 79 *Sandgelb* or RLM 76 *Lichtblau* as illustrated by E8+CH, which featured the reduced 1/5th size unit i/d codes (EH), with standard sized individual aircraft letter (C) and *Staffel* letter (H), and the 'open' style national markings on the wing upper surfaces, fuselage and fin. These night harassment aircraft were also fitted with large flame damping exhaust pipes.

Junkers Ju 87G-1, GS+MD of 10.(Pz) SG 1, Orsha, eastern Belarus, late 1944/early 1945 | In October 1943, the Luftwaffe re-designated its Stuka units as *Schlachtgeschwader* (SG, Ground-Attack Groups) to better reflect the Stuka's change in tactics from pure dive-bombing to more generalised ground attack operations and as such, StG 1 became SG 1. Around the same time, a developed variant of the Stuka was introduced, the Ju 87G-1, based upon the D-1, armed with a pair of underwing-mounted 37mm Flak 18 cannon, which were allocated to newly formed independent *staffeln* who specialised in the anti-tank role, such as 10.(Pz) SG 1. Many of these G-1s were rushed into service straight from the factory and the units didn't have time to apply their codes so they were operated still carrying the *stammkennzeichen* factory codes, like GS+MD, which also had a white mirror-wave/meander scribble pattern 'snow' scheme over the standard RLM 70/71 upper surfaces.

Junkers Ju 87G-2, *werknummer* 494193 of *Stab* SG 2, Seregélyes, central Hungary, February 1945, flown by *Oberst* Hans-Ulrich Rudel, SG 2's *Geschwader Kommodore* | A more refined variant of the 37mm Flak 18 cannon-armed 'Gustav', the G-2, was based upon the longer wingspan D-5. No book on the 'Stuka' would be complete without an illustration of one of Hans-Ulrich Rudel's machines, and this particular aircraft, WNr 494193, flown by him during late 1944/early 1945, with black chevron and bar markings outlined in white on the fuselage and a white spinner with a black spiral, is the one in which he was shot down on 8 February 1945, resulting in his right leg being amputated below the knee. Incredibly, he returned to flying on 25 March 1945, and claimed a further twenty-six tanks destroyed before the end of the war, bringing his final total to 519, plus over 800 vehicles, and a battleship, in a total of 2,530 combat missions.

Junkers Ju 87B-2 of 209ª *Squadriglia*, 97° *Gruppo*, *Regia Aeronautica*, flown by Capitano Romanesi, Balkan Campaign, April 1941 | The Ju 87B/Rs, were referred to as the *'Picchiatelli'* by the *Regia Aeronautica* – from *'picchiatello'* an Italian cartoon character, the 'Little Woodpecker', which loosely translated as 'crazy diver/dive bomber'. All were finished in the standard RLM 70/71/65 scheme, with the Luftwaffe national markings painted out and a white 'Savoy Cross', painted on the rudder and fin, with the *fasci* national insignia under the wings – no markings were carried above the wings. Most of the *Regia Aeronautica's* B/Rs that operated in the campaigns in Yugoslavia, Greece and Albania, featured a yellow band around the mid cowling with a white Mediterranean Theatre band around the rear fuselage as illustrated. Operating as semi-autonomous units, generally just the *Squadriglia* identification number (209) was applied, on the fuselage sides, in this case in yellow, with an individual aircraft number (in this case '10') on the front of the spats, also in yellow.

Junkers Ju 87A-1, B.6+04, of *Stukaschule* 2, 3/1 *Bombazo Osztaly*, Royal Hungarian Air Force, Borogond, Hungary, mid-1942 | In March 1942, three Ju 87A-1s were delivered to the Royal Hungarian Air Force (*Magyar Királyi Honvéd Légierő*, MKHL). Finished in the RLM 70/71/65 scheme, with Hungarian black square with white-cross national markings which had been introduced in late 1941/early 1942, the aircraft were assigned to *Stukaschule* 2 (2nd Dive Bomber School), 3/1 *Bombazo Osztaly* (Bomber Group 3/1) for dive bomber training duties. The markings applied to the fuselage and wings were enlivened by the red/white/green Hungarian national colours in broad bands across the fin and rudder and both surfaces of the tailplanes. The four-character code, B.604, was applied on the fuselage in yellow, and a yellow Eastern Front theatre band was carried around the rear fuselage. The wing tip under surfaces were also yellow as was the propeller spinner tip.

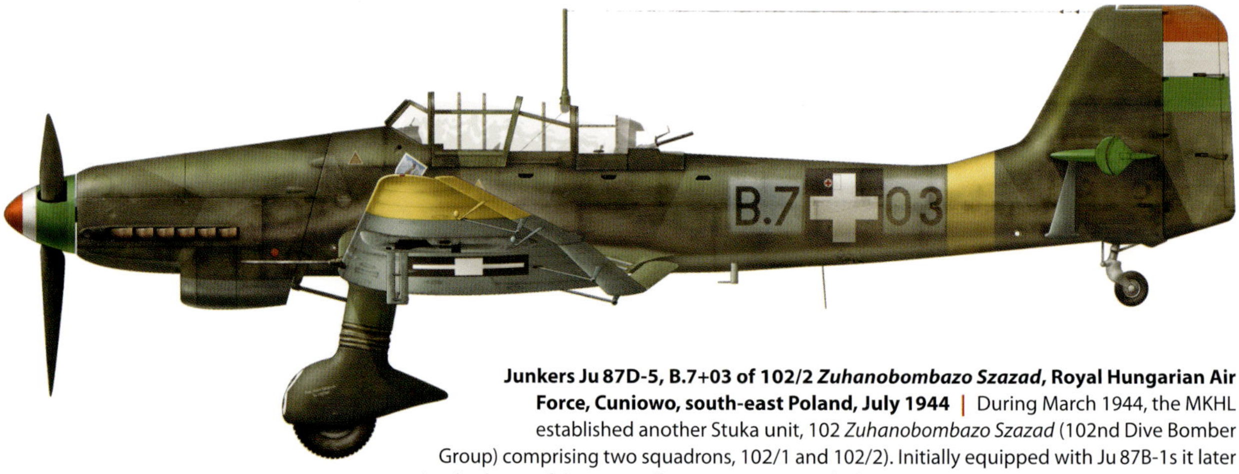

Junkers Ju 87D-5, B.7+03 of 102/2 *Zuhanobombazo Szazad*, Royal Hungarian Air Force, Cuniowo, south-east Poland, July 1944 | During March 1944, the MKHL established another Stuka unit, 102 *Zuhanobombazo Szazad* (102nd Dive Bomber Group) comprising two squadrons, 102/1 and 102/2). Initially equipped with Ju 87B-1s it later received a dozen of the more effective D-5 variant of which B.703 was one. Finished in the standard RLM 70/71/65 scheme, the Luftwaffe markings were painted out and replaced with the MKHL markings, with the tips of the tailplanes, the top of the rudder and the propeller spinner carrying the red/white/green Hungarian national colours in broad bands. The four-character code, B.703, was applied over areas of (possibly) RLM 76 where the original Luftwaffe codes had been. The unit's coconut throwing monkey badge was carried below the windscreen, and a yellow Eastern Front band was applied around the rear fuselage and the wing tip under surfaces were yellow.

Junkers Ju 87D-3, '9', of *Grupul 3° Bombardement Picaj*, Royal Romanian Air Force, Bagherovo, Crimea, summer 1943, crewed by *Adj* Alfons Aunero (pilot) and *Caporal* Viorel Almăsanu | The *Forțele Aeriene Regale ale României* (Royal Romanian Air Force, FARR), obtained its Stukas during the summer of 1943 when the first of some forty-five D-3s were handed over from Luftwaffe stocks. Equipping *Grupul* 3° *Bombardement Picaj* (No 3 Bomber Group), the unit first saw action over the Kerch Peninsular in Russia during July. Finished in the standard RLM 70/71/65 scheme, all the Luftwaffe markings were painted out and Romanian 'Michael the Brave' cross markings added. Yellow fuselage bands and wing tip undersides were also added. This particular 'Dora' had the words '*Hai Pusa*', (Come on Pusha), written on the cowling in white and the numeral '9' on the top of the rudder.

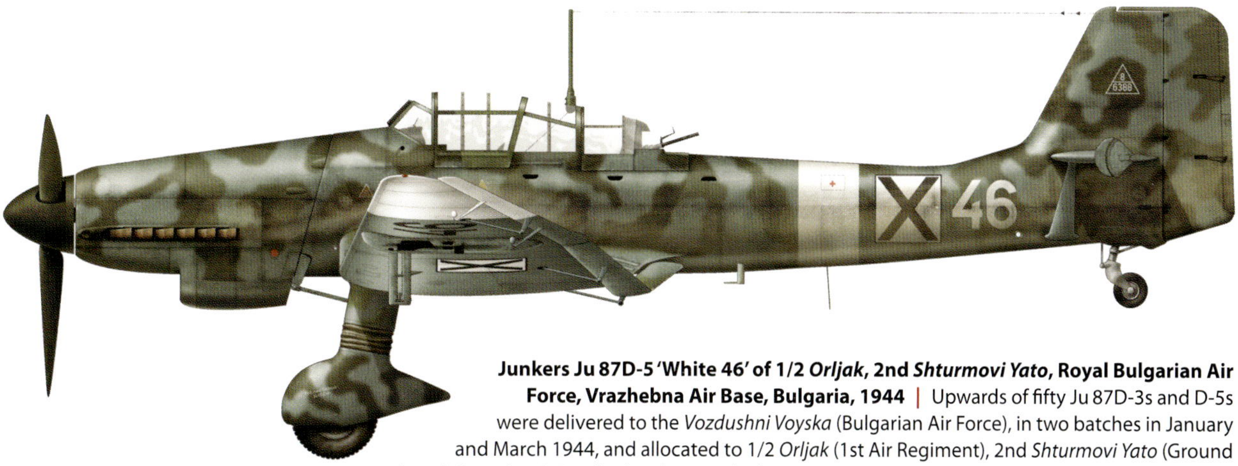

Junkers Ju 87D-5 'White 46' of 1/2 *Orljak*, 2nd *Shturmovi Yato*, Royal Bulgarian Air Force, Vrazhebna Air Base, Bulgaria, 1944 | Upwards of fifty Ju 87D-3s and D-5s were delivered to the *Vozdushni Voyska* (Bulgarian Air Force), in two batches in January and March 1944, and allocated to 1/2 *Orljak* (1st Air Regiment), 2nd *Shturmovi Yato* (Ground Attack Squadron). Finished in the standard RLM 70/71/65 scheme, all the Luftwaffe markings were painted out and black saltire crosses on white square markings were applied on both surfaces of the wings and the fuselage sides. Yellow Eastern Front bands were applied in front of the fuselage cross, and yellow wing tip under surfaces, but when Bulgaria changed sides in September 1944 to operate with Soviet forces, the yellow fuselage band and wingtips were overpainted in white. At some stage random areas of RLM 76 *Lichtblau* were applied over the upper surfaces of '46' and possibly other Bulgarian 'Doras' too.

Junkers Ju 87B-2, ex-5B+ER of *Stab*/NSGr 10, Karmasc, Yugoslavia, captured and operated by Yugoslav partisan forces, April 1945 | At least one Ju 87B was captured by partisan forces in Yugoslavia and used against its previous owners. An ex-*Nachtschlachtgruppe* 10 aircraft, it retained its RLM 70/71 and 65 scheme and green (*Stab* colour) spinner, but the yellow Eastern Front Theatre markings appear to have been overpainted, possibly with grey paint. The aircraft carried full Yugoslav insurgent markings albeit roughly applied, with the underwing star markings painted on white square backgrounds, presumably covering the original Luftwaffe *balkenkreuze*.

Modelling the Stuka

In starting this Flight Craft title, we expected there would have been 'quite a few' Stuka kits produced over the years, but perhaps not quite as many as there actually were! Having said that, some of the kits are the same moulds merely repackaged by different companies and released and marketed under the various manufacturers' names with different box-top artwork.

Some of the kits date back several years and many of course are no longer generally available, but where we have been able to find details of the kits in question, either from our own collections, or more usually from the collections of our modelling friends and acquaintances, we have added explanatory and/or appropriate notes accordingly. Inevitably, however, several of the kits listed here contain more detailed information than others, but, where only the barest detail appears, it represents the sum of any information unearthed.

AHM 1/144 scale

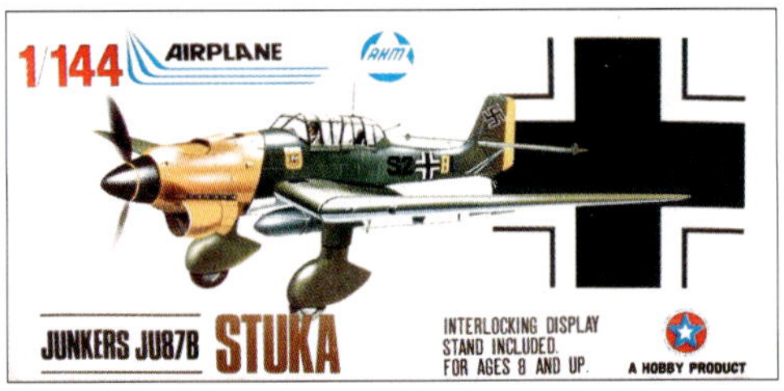

EDUARD 1/144 scale

Eduard's 1/144th scale Stukas by Mike Verier – IPMS 1/144 Scale Special Interest Group

There are several Ju 87s available in 1/144 scale, but by far the best are Eduard's. First produced in 2004 they have since been re-released as two-in-a-box 'Combos'.

There are two basic toolings – for a Ju 87B and a Ju 87G, both of which offer crisp and accurate replicas of the Stuka, with different engine cowlings, cockpit canopies and wings all accounted for. Being Eduard you also get brass etch for the (different) tailplane struts, dive brakes, machine guns, aerials, and bomb release crutch. In the case of the 'G' the etch includes ammunition trays for the BK 37 anti-tank cannon. There is also a mask provided for various markings (but not the canopy).

The Ju 87B tooling was also released as an 'R' – the two drop tanks remain on the common sprue so you still have the option for a standard 'B'.

Decals are excellent and offer three different schemes for each sub-type; all told an excellent package. Despite this the toolings date from a time when cockpits were not considered important for 1/144th scale and, indeed, there isn't one – just a flat shelf to stand the canopy on!

Models as good as this however attract the attention of the aftermarket and Retrokit have solved this problem with a quite superb resin cockpit which transforms the model at very modest cost. Recently Retrokit released a conversion set for the folding wing Ju 87C intended for the *Kreigsmarine*'s never-completed aircraft carrier. OWL produce alternative resin 'un-spatted' wheels (a common feature of Stukas on the Eastern Front) and have announced replacement flying surfaces too. Also available from OWL are detailed resin replacements for the BK 37s and just to prove that anything can be improved upon, Master have produced stunning turned brass gun barrels for them.

Ju 87B (4414) New tool in 2004

Ju 87R (4415) 2004
Ju 87B with changed parts

Ju 87D (4416) 2004

Ju 87G (4417) 2004
Ju 87D with changed parts

Ju 87G Dual Combo (4430) 2014
Changed decals

Ju 87B Dual Combo (4431) 2014
Changed decals

GUNZE SANGYO

1/144 scale

Ju 87B Stuka (H-1019) 1973

HORNET

1/144 scale

'Miniwing Series'
Ju 87A-1 Stuka (Mini004)

MITSUWA MODEL

1/144 scale

Ju 87B Stuka (1011)

REVELL

1/144 scale

Ju 87B Stuka (H-1019) 1973

Ju 87B Stuka (4047) 1992
Changed boxtop

'Micro-Wings' Ju 87B Stuka (04918) 2012
Changed decals

ZVEZDA

1/144 scale

Ju 87B-2 Stuka (6123) 2010
The exact opposite of the Eduard approach, the Zvezda Ju 87 is the right shape but is intended for the Wargame market and as such is very simplified with just six parts. Decals are generic crosses and numbers. The work required to bring this anywhere near a detailed model probably outweighs its low cost. **Mike Verier**

ACADEMY 1/72 scale

Ju 87G-1 (1641 & 12450)
Ju 87G-2 (12404 & 12539)

The Academy Ju 87G-1 (1641), released in 2001, (and subsequently re-released in 2010 as 12450) features the short-span wings of the D-1/D-3 series, upon which the G-1 was based. The kit looks impressive in the box with crisp, finely engraved panel lines, thin clear parts and decent detail, but is rumoured to be a little short in the nose area. Another shortcoming is the propeller assembly – the diameter of the propeller is significantly undersized and the spinner looks too blunt, possibly adding to the 'short nose' impression. The compression boots on the undercarriage legs appear to be too long, although the spats themselves seem to be the right dimensions. A pair of 37mm anti-tank cannon are included, which are well done.

Academy's Ju 87G-2, released in 2005 (12404) and again in 2016 (as 12539) is essentially the same kit, but was released with retooled wings to reflect the correct 'longer span' with extended wingtips of the G-2. This kit also features a pair of underwing 37mm cannon. As might be expected in this scale, some of the subtler elements are oversimplified, which include the machine guns in the rear of the cockpit and the hinge arrangement for the flaps/ailerons. Markings are provided for one aircraft, a Ju 87G-2 flown by the commander of StG 2, Major Hans-Ulrich Rudel in the summer of 1944 over the Russian Front.

Academy's Ju 87B-2 (kit number 72001) was released in 2008, and may originally be from a HobbyCraft mould that HobbyCraft never actually released. Apparently they were getting ready to release a Ju 87B kit, but for whatever reason didn't, and it would appear that Academy acquired the mould (as Academy produced the master moulds for HobbyCraft kits at that time anyway), and released the kit themselves, as a Ju 87B-2/Trop.

AIRFIX 1/72 scale

Airfix have released four Stuka kits in 1/72 scale to date – a Ju 87B in 1957, two Ju 87B/Rs in the late 1970s, and more recently a superb new tooling in 2016. The 1950s kit, (1395-91-01011), the eleventh aircraft kit produced by Airfix, can be discounted for all but avid historical kit collectors, as not only was it slightly undersize, it was very much a product of its time and is somewhat crude and very basic by today's standards (although much loved by modellers of 'a certain age' who were youngsters then!)

In November 1978 Airfix released a rather nice Ju 87B/R in their Series 3 Range, (03030 - 02049), which was followed a year later in November 1979, by a 'straight' Ju 87B in a Series 2 box, (02049 - 01067), which was a simplified version of the Series 3 Ju 87B/R kit. The same patterns were used but some previously multi-part items were re-tooled as single parts, including the mainwheels and wheel spats which were moulded as one. The cockpit interior was also simplified.

Outline accuracy (for both toolings) was generally good, apparently benefiting from the research done for the company's 1/24 scale kit, (see the end of this section), although all panel lines and rivets were raised, plus there was a general lack of cockpit detail compared to more recent manufacturers' offerings. The canopies show all the framing as external, whereas in reality some was internal, (i.e. inside the Perspex and therefore not camouflage coloured). Both late 1970s kits also feature the 'square' carburettor intake moulded on the fuselage side, essentially making them tropicalised versions.

When Hornby purchased Airfix in 2006, they started a programme of revamping many older subjects and issuing newly-tooled kits – the Ju 87B being a case in point. In 2016 Airfix released a brand-new CAD-design tool Ju 87B-1 (A03087), a good choice as almost twice as many B-1s were built compared to the B-2.

The kit is typical of Airfix's most recent CAD design releases, moulded in pale grey plastic with delicately engraved panel lines and detail. It is well engineered and it is obvious from the way the parts are arranged that Airfix have plans for other variants to be kitted.

The cockpit interior is well detailed, with separate sidewall parts, an instrument panel for which there is a decal supplied for the dials, a choice of pilot seats – one with belt detail and the other without so that the pilot figure can fit more easily – a cockpit floor that includes short spars to help with the wing build sequence. Holes need to be opened in the wing undersides for the outer bomb racks if required, and 300-litre drop tanks are included so that a Ju 87R-1 can be completed.

The major external difference between the B-1 and the B-2 was the engine cowling, and as such Airfix have moulded this kit's nose parts with the variant's stub exhausts and more rounded upper intake. The nose is built up as a separate 'power egg' to be attached to the rest of the airframe – the nose and propeller parts are on a separate sprue, allowing for a B-2/R-2 (and possibly even a D and G series in the fullness of time) to be released in the future. The propeller assembly, featuring the correct narrow propeller blades, can be assembled and installed after the rest of the kit is built and painted. The mainwheels have 'flats' moulded on for realistic ground display, but if you wish to portray the model 'in flight', you can simply rotate the wheels to hide the 'flats' inside the spats. Although not shown in the instructions, there is also the option of adding stubs to the undercarriage legs to accommodate its wind-driven propeller sirens.

The aileron and flap assembly are single, full-span pieces, that include integrally-moulded control linkages and aileron mass balances. For the main centreline bomb load, there is a choice between a 500kg and a 250kg bomb for which different bomb crutches are provided, four 50kg bombs beneath the wings and single piece dive brakes. There are two central canopy sections provided for 'open' and 'closed' main canopy hoods.

The instructions are well printed with colour areas to assist with building the kit. Decal options, are also well printed (albeit without swastikas), and feature a Spanish Civil War, 5 *Staffel*, *Kampfgruppe* 88 machine and a 9 *Staffel* StG 51 machine based in France in August 1940.

FROG 1/72 scale

Ju 87G (F195)

This was a new tool released in 1968, and subsequently marketed by UPC in 1969 (5053), Hasegawa in 1970 (JS 044) and again in 1971 (with the same JS 044 catalogue number) and re-released by Frog in 1975 (F181).

FUJIMI

1/72 scale

Fujimi's range of Ju 87 kits were initially released in the mid-1980s. They were very expensive and quite difficult to obtain at the time. All were well packaged and moulded in light grey plastic with good surface detail. The canopies can only be displayed in the closed position, unlike most of the newer Stuka kits, and interior detail is quite minimal at best. However, even straight out-of-the-box, the kits built up well and with a little extra work could be built into very nice models.

Ju 87B/R (F-13)
Reboxed by Astrokit (72101)

Ju 87B-1 'Shark Mouth' (F-17 / 35133)
Initially released in the late 1980s, based upon the B/R it offered alternative exhausts for an early B-1.

Ju 87D-1/D-3 (F-14 / 25014)

Ju 87G-1 (F-15)

Ju 87D-5 (F-16)
This kit, with its long-span wings, can made into either a D-5 or a D-8. The canopy on this kit is a single piece and a bit thick but quite clear. Weapons include a centreline bomb as well as under wing bomb racks with smaller bombs. Decals are for two aircraft, both from the Russian front. At the time this kit was probably the best 1/72 Ju 87 on the market.

Ju 87G-2 (F-17, later 72061)
Re-boxed by Testors (342)

HELLER

1/72 scale

Ju 87B (80388)
Originally released in 1972, the kit was well detailed for the time but like the original 1957 Airfix kit was slightly under scale at 1/75 (?) Subsequently re-released in 1976, 1979, 1986 and the early 1990s, the kit is no longer available and has been superseded by superior 1/72 scale kits.

HOBBYBOSS

1/72 scale

Ju 87D-3 (80286)
As with most 'easy assembly' kits in this series, the model is simplified with just forty-six light grey and three clear-plastic parts. As such, the lower fuselage incorporates the full span one-piece wings and the upper fuselage has the fin moulded integrally. The outline is basically accurate, and the kit is designed to go together easily with little trimming.

The cockpit interior tub is in with the upper fuselage section, and the pilot's seat, control column and the rear *zwilling* machine gun mount is simply inserted into the tub. There is a decal for the instrument panel, although it doesn't fit exactly to the shape of the panel. No rear gunner's seat is provided and no sidewall detail. There are no aileron mass balances or pitot tube, although a clear disc for the DF antenna in the upper fuselage is supplied.

The tailplane is trapped between the fuselage halves and other parts like the tailplane braces, underwing radiator housings, flaps and ailerons, spatted landing gear and what appears to be an 1,800kg bomb, with appropriate crutch, are attached separately. Unfortunately, the kit is wrongly identified as it has the long-span wings introduced on the D-5. The D-3 had standard span wings, plus dive brakes and wing racks for bombs, none of which are included. The kit includes a pair of BK 3.7cm, Flak 18 *kanonenvogel* underwing-mounted cannon – which were used by the Ju 87G! However, these are not totally accurate as they lack the ammunition feeds that protruded from each side of the gun pods.

Unlike many other HobbyBoss kits, this one has separate tailwheel and exhaust stacks and the wing-mounted 20mm MG 151/20 cannon barrels are separate items as well. There is a one-piece canopy and the clear bomb-aiming window in the lower forward fuselage is also included. While the propeller spinner appears to be the proper shape, the blades look too short.

There are decals for two aircraft, both with StG 77 – one in the standard RLM 70/71/65 scheme with a yellow fuselage band and outer underside wing tips; the other in a similar scheme but with a white winter camouflage on the upper surfaces. Swastikas are included, but printed in four separate parts.

ITALERI 1/72 scale

Ju 87B-2/R2 (079, 6805 and 1292)
Originally released in 1997 (079), this kit was re-released in 1999 (6805) and again in 2010 (1292). We couldn't find any details other than the decal options, which comprised:

- **Ju 87B-2**, T6+MP, 6./StG 2 in Libya, January 1942
- **Ju 87R-2**, S1+CK, 2./StG 3, Crete May 1941
- **Ju 87B-2**, F1+LR, 7./StG 77, France August 1940
- **Ju 87R-2**, *Regia Aeronautica*, Greece December 1940

The kit was reboxed by Revell in 2002 (04620) and by Tamiya in 2007 (60776)

Ju 87D-5 (070) 1997, (1070) 2005

Ju 87G-2 (1221) 2001 – D-5 with new parts (reboxed by Zvezda in 2010 (7261)

MATCHBOX 1/72 scale

Ju 87G-1/D-3

This kit was released *circa* 1976 (PK-111) and re-released with new box tops in 1978 and 1982, and then again in the mid-1980s. No longer generally available, it was a typical Matchbox product, in multi-coloured plastic parts with deeply engraved panel lines, but built up in to an acceptably accurate kit. It featured optional standard and long-span outer wing panels with appropriate ailerons, a separate rudder, optional bomb load, for which dive brakes were provided, and 37mm underwing cannon. This kit was also marketed by Tamiya in Japan.

MPM 1/72 scale

Released in the mid-1990s, it was one of MPM's first injection-moulded kits, (previously they had only produced vacforms). It is typical of their first short-run kits, moulded in dark brown plastic with traces of flash and a slightly rough surface texture, although the panel line detail is crisply engraved, albeit very shallow. The interior has a floor, central bulkhead, control column, seats, instrument panel and a rearward-firing machine gun, although no sidewall detail is provided. No etch brass for seat belts etc. is included. No bomb, or cradle is included, although dive brakes are. A single, somewhat thick and slightly cloudy vacformed canopy is provided. Instructions are quite basic with a brief history, parts layout, exploded diagram construction details and a decal and colour scheme guide three view. Two Luftwaffe schemes are shown, but no swastika as such, just a small black square. (see Special Hobby Ju 87A opposite)

REVELL 1/72 scale

Ju 87B/R (0149)

First released in 1981, and then re-boxed with different decal options in 2002 (04620).

Ju 87G

It is thought that the Revell Ju 87G kit might be a re-boxing of the old Frog toolings. The four sprues of dark green plastic, featuring some sixty parts, have raised panel lines (although these are quite delicate) with a little flash here and there that require some cleaning-up. The single piece canopy is thick although clear enough.

As might be expected from nearly 50-year old moulds, detail is a little soft compared to modern Revell kits. The two decal options include markings for a Ju 87G-2 of 10.(Pz)/StG 3, Jakobstadt, Lettland, July 1944; and a Ju 87D-3 of 4./StG 2, Russia 1944 (although only long-span wing tips are provided).

SPECIAL HOBBY 1/72 scale

Ju 87A-1

This is Special Hobby's second attempt at the Ju 87A, the first being one of their very early releases under the MPM label (see above). Although it is a new tool mould, up to Special Hobby's/MPM's current standards of detailing and parts crispness, some of the smaller parts are very 'chunky' and it will take some modelling skill to complete. Despite not being a particularly easy model to build, the kit does make in to a reasonable model. A few of the smaller interior parts are resin and the etch brass sheet has items such as dive brakes, belts and rear-gunner's seat along with several other small interior bits. The propeller blades are in one piece, but no bombs are included. The single-piece canopy is injected moulded plastic and is quite clear so any interior work will be visible. Markings are for three Luftwaffe machines – from StG 102 based in Bohemia/Moravia, 1943/44 with yellow fuselage band and lower wing tips; a training school in 1940, also with yellow lower wing tips; and a pre-war 'Anton' attached to 4./StG 165 in mid-1938. Decals are well printed and have two-part swastikas.

IMAI 1/50 scale

Ju 87B

An old Japanese kit dating back to the late-1960s/early 1970s. It is no longer available. It was, apparently, well moulded (for its time) and included a separate rudder and elevators, a bomb cradle that swung the bomb clear of the propeller arc, an elevating rear gun and a sliding canopy. The kit came with all the hardware for motorizing, although the Mabuchi Baby Motor was not included and had to be purchased separately.

AIRFIX 1/48 scale

Ju 87B-2/R-2 (A05100)

Originally released in 1981 (05100-4), the kit was re-released with various box top illustrations in 1983 (9 05100), 1991 (05100) and in 2010 (A05100). It was also released by Heller in 1992, as part of the Airfix/Heller trading deal, with additional parts such as etch brass detail set and white metal exposed undercarriage legs.

The kit comprises almost 90 parts, on three light grey sprues and one clear sprue (bagged separately). All the surface detailing is raised, including the panel lines and rows of fine rivet heads. The fuselage halves have raised internal detail with a cockpit floor, instrument panel, gun/bomb-sight, control column, pilot and gunner's seats, radio boxes and rear bulkhead, which at the time was more than adequate and can still pass muster with a decent interior paint job. The engine cowling top is separate and the exhaust manifolds are integrally moulded in with the cowling sides and underslung radiator fairing. The canopy is in two sections, windscreen and pilot's hood, and the central section with the gunner's hood, with delicately moulded raised framing. There is also a clear, underfuselage, dive-bombing window.

The wings are in port and starboard, upper and under-surface halves, with separate full length aileron/flaps which are glued to the trailing edges via stub 'hinges', after which separate actuators and horn balances are added creating a reasonably acceptable, if not totally realistic, but sturdy option. The main undercarriage spats are in halves, with spindles designed to trap the mainwheel

hubs before joining, but with a little gentle prising, the mainwheels can be painted and added into the spats after the airframe has been painted. Underwing dive brakes are separate, although the underwing ETC 50 bomb racks are integrally moulded. The propeller unit has separate blades, (the broader B-2/R-2 'laminated wood' VS 5 style), which locate at the correct angle on to a back plate with a separate spinner cap.

Offensive bomb load comprises a single SC 250 bomb and appropriate underfuselage bomb cradle, and four SC 50 bombs for the ETC 50 underwing bomb racks. Alternatively, two 300-litre fuel tanks are provided for the R-2 version.

Decal choices varied depending upon the various release dates and boxtop changes – e.g. the 1991 boxing included a B-2 from III./StG 3, North Africa early 1942, and an R-2 from III./StG 2, Eastern Front 1941.

Despite its age the kit still builds into a reasonably acceptable representation of the Stuka – an oldie but a goody, although it doesn't appear to be currently unavailable.

Ju 87B-1 (A07114)

A brand-new CAD-designed kit, released in January 2017, this second 1/48 scale Stuka produced by Airfix, (see above), features the Ju 87B-1 variant. Packaged in a large box with over 170 mid-grey parts all bagged together (some of which aren't needed for this B-1 version), and nine clear plastic parts in their own bag, all are cleanly moulded with a good surface finish and neatly engraved panel lines, rivets and inspection hatches.

The kit faithfully reflects the subtle differences of the B-1's underslung radiator intake, with separate fixed cooling gills and slightly different shaped 'curves' on the upper cowling intake. The B-1/R-1's narrower metal propeller blades are included (plus the B-2/R-2s broader 'laminated wood' VS 5 propeller blades – presumably for a future release) and the early production B-1/R-1's small oval exhaust manifolds, (Later production B-1s and R-1s had ejector exhaust manifolds, similar to the B-2s, which are not included).

There is a well detailed multi-part Jumo engine provided, which has optional parts if the modeller wants to build the model with it fitted and maybe displayed with the cowlings left off. Amongst other features, there is a choice of full-span flaps and ailerons, either neutrally balanced or with dropped flaps and angled ailerons, both with integrally moulded, and very delicate, aileron and flap control linkages and aileron horn balances, which, despite being protected by the sprue frames, are prone to getting bent and even knocked off in the box.

A design trend is becoming apparent with these new Airfix kits whereby the cockpit floor is built as part of a wing spar section which, in this case, also forms the boxed-in compartments for the forward-firing machine guns, ensuring the inverted gull wing mainplanes maintain their correct anhedral/dihedral. The cockpit interior is well detailed, comprising some twenty parts with the side-frames featuring good moulded detail. The radios look good and the instrument panel is moulded in such a way that it can either be totally hand painted with dials etc. picked out with a fine brush, or by using the decal sheet provided. Strangely, no gun/bomb-sight is included. Given that one was provided in their new 1/72 scale kit we presume this is a design oversight in 1/48 scale! No seat straps for the crew are provided either, however, there is a plentiful supply of ammunition drums for the gunner/radio operator whose frame-style swivel seat is somewhat over-intricately moulded in several parts. As the kit can be mounted on a stand (available separately), it's a little surprising that no crew figures are included.

The wings are built up from five parts – an underside centre-section that mounts onto the previously mentioned wing spar section, which includes the undercarriage mounts; a pair of underside outer wing panels; and a pair of upperwing halves. The tail surfaces feature a separate rudder and elevators – a clever touch being that different endplates are provided – one set for neutrally positioned elevators and the other for deflected elevators, either 'up' or 'down' depending upon which way up the end plates are glued on to the tailplanes.

There is an option to model the undercarriage legs in the compressed 'under weight', or fully extended 'flying' positions, by simply cutting off a marked section off the upper 'trouser leg' section for the 'under weight option'. The mainwheels are moulded with 'under weight' tyres, which can be rotated and fitted at the appropriate angle in the spats for either 'weighted' or 'un-weighted' tyres effect.

Location holes need to be opened in the wing under surfaces for the ETC 50 bomb racks before the wing halves are assembled, and there is an option to display the wing gun bays open, but it is left to the modeller to cut open and remove the panels, carefully, as surprisingly, there aren't any guide cutting lines on the inside to follow. Parts for the MG 17 breeches, mounting brackets and

ammunition belt feed are provided, if the 'open' option is taken, and while simple, are suitably effective. External stores comprise a 500kg and a 250kg bomb, with appropriate under fuselage swing crutch, and four underwing 50kg bombs. The main bombs have commendably thin fins, but lack the support braces for them.

The canopy parts are thin and clear, with the centre section in two styles – either 'closed', or with the pilot's canopy slid back over it – making it a challenge to paint the frame lines in the latter position as paint will have to be applied from the inside. The gunner's MG 17 fits into a separate circular mount that can be swivelled in to any position.

Assembly instructions are clearly presented in a 20-page A4 booklet with easy to follow diagrams and although the painting guide, unsurprisingly, only quotes Humbrol paints, RLM codes/colours are also given. Decals are included for two aircraft, both finished in the RLM 70/71/65 camouflage scheme: Ju 87B-1 of I./StG 2, Bonn-Hangelar, Germany, spring 1940; and a B-1, of *Kampfgruppe* 88, Condor Legion, Spain 1938. No swastikas are included for the StG 2 scheme, but aftermarket items are easily obtainable.

ITALERI 1/48 scale

Ju 87B-2 (2690)

First released in 2010 and, at the time of writing, still generally available. We understand that it is to be re-released and reboxed as a *Regia Aeronautica* B-2/R-2 *Picchiatello* (2769) at some point in 2017. The kit comes in an envelope-style box with a tray inside, the box top illustration depicting a machine of III./StG 77 *Stab* with yellow nose and rudder, with photographs of the sprues and illustrations of the four decal schemes on the back.

When this kit was first released, many thought it was re-boxing of the Hasegawa kit, but it **is** an all new tool moulding, comprising about 160 parts on six pale grey and one clear sprues, with a small photo-etched fret for the instrument panel, seat belts, part of the observer's seat, and the tailplane/elevator end plates. All the parts have finely engraved surface detail. The cockpit interior has detailed sidewalls and floor and there's a choice for the main instrument panel – either use the instrument decals provided straight over the plastic part, or use the etched brass panel with the instrument decals behind it.

The canopy parts are thin and crystal clear, with well-defined framework, and come in four sections which allows the pilot's hood to be displayed slid back and 'open'. Parts for a commendably complete Jumo engine are included, (virtually a kit in its own right). The separate engine cowling is in sections, to be assembled around the completed engine, with the cowling top designed to fit so that the model can be displayed with or without the engine visible.

The wings consist of a single, full span underside, complete with integrally-moulded flaps and ailerons, and two upperwing halves. The undercarriage legs/spats are in halves and have fittings for the 'sirens. The mainwheels have 'flats' moulded on the tyres and separate dive brakes are included. The tailplanes have separate elevators and the rudder is separate. A selection of 250kg and 50kg bombs and 300ltr long range drop tanks are included.

The decal sheet is good and includes four B-2s – from 7./StG 1, 1940; 2./St.G 2, August 1940; *Stab* 3./StG 77, April 1941; and 2./St.G 2, July 1941 – plus a number of stencils for the airframe and the bombs. Although the decal placement instructions are rather

poor as other than the larger markings, they contain no visual clue as to where to place most of the smaller markings and modellers are left to their own devices to ensure everything is correctly placed and orientated.

These moulds were also marketed under the Tamiya label as 'Ju 87B-2 w/Bomb Loading Set' (37008) in 2011 (see later).

Ju 87D-5 (2709)

Generally based upon the toolings for the B-2/R-2, (above), the D-5 features new sprues and parts appropriate for the D-5, which include the long-span wings, again consisting of a single, full span underside, complete with integrally-moulded flaps and ailerons and two upperwing halves. The undercarriage legs/spats correctly represent the re-designed style and a new three-part 'streamlined' nose cowling is included, that also fits around the engine.

Other new parts specific to the D-5 include slight changes for the cockpit interior including an armoured headrest for the pilot, different machine gun magazines, a new rear decking section with a clear disc

cover for the Peil G IV radio ranging device, re-contoured clear canopy, again in four parts, MG 81Z rearward firing machine guns, underwing radiators, multi-purpose ETC 50 rack fairings, wing-mounted MG 151 20mm cannon barrels and pipe-like flame dampers to fit over the exhaust manifolds. The propeller blades and back plate are the same but the spinner is the slightly more pointed style but doesn't look totally accurate, being a little too 'blunt'.

Offensive ordnance is the same as the B-2/R-2 but the instructions suggest the fitting of the AB Light Weapons Dispensers that were included but 'blanked off' on the B-2/R-2 kit's instructions. Decal choices include Ju 87D-5s from *Stab* StG 3, Finland 1944; *Stab* III./SG 2, Russia 1943/44; 1./NSG 9, Italy 1944, and a Hungarian Air Force machine, Ukraine 1943.

Ju 87G-2 *Kanonenvogel* (2722)
Basically the Ju 87D-5 kit, which Italeri released in 2013 with parts for the BK 37 anti-tank cannon and alternative parts for the main undercarriage to be modelled either with, or without, the 'spats'.

HASEGAWA 1/48 scale

Hasegawa have been producing 1/48 scale Stuka kits since the 1990s, and the range includes an array of Ju 87B/Rs, Cs, Ds and Gs. They were one of the first manufacturers to make extensive use of modular design and drop-in mould sections to create multiple versions from a core set of parts. So, like the full-sized aircraft, the kits share many of the same basic airframe parts with the first sub-type they released, the Ju 87B in 1994.

Ju 87B-2/R-2
Comprising some 120 light grey and seven clear plastic parts the overall general outline of the kit is good and construction is straightforward. Surface detail is typical Hasegawa, very smooth (there are no visible rivets) with delicately engraved panel lines. The cockpit interior is more than adequately detailed with a cockpit floor, instrument panel, rudder pedals, control column, pilot's seat, armoured headrest, radio boxes, gunner's seat, ammunition box and separate panels with sidewall detail. There is also a bomb aiming window in the floor in front of the pilot.

The nose cowling is separate and made up of multiple parts, with separate exhaust manifolds that can be pre-painted and added after the rest of the airframe is painted. The propeller spinner and the separate VS 5 blades are well-shaped and fit without problems. The clear cockpit canopy is in four sections and with a little care the pilot's hood can be posed 'open'.

The wings come in two upper halves, with a full span lower half that has the distinctive ailerons and flaps moulded integrally along the trailing edge, which might be bemoaned by purists, but the average modeller may well welcome the simplicity it offers. When the completed wing assembly is joined to the fuselage a little care is needed to make sure that the fuselage wing roots and wing upper surfaces are level and don't end up with a bit of a step.

The undercarriage spats are in halves that are joined to an upper fairing that slots into the wing underside to create a positive join. With care the mainwheels can be prised into the spats after all the painting is complete.

Offensive armament includes a centreline-mounted SC 250 bomb with separate fins and bomb trapeze crutch and four SC 50 bombs and ETC 50 racks beneath the wings. In the Ju 87R-2 boxings, a pair of 300-litre drop tanks are also included on separate sprues. Decal choices abound in the various boxings that Hasegawa have released over the years.

The same mouldings were released by Revell in 2001, Ju 87B-2 (04564) the only differences being the decal options, which included T6+CP of 6./StG 2 with a 'snake' along the fuselage sides, and F1+BC of 3./StG 77.

Ju 87B-2 'Stuka w/Skid' (07317)
This is one of the many 'special boxing' kits. In this case it is the standard Ju 87B kit with a set of resin skis. The resin parts are well moulded and are simple replacements for the wheels. In case you just can't make up your mind, the fit of the wheels in the spats is so tight you don't have to glue them in and could easily make them interchangeable.

The kit's decal options, DJ+KA and DJ+FU, may be in error as apparently the three Ju 87Bs that were fitted with skis were the earlier B-1 versions and while they were fitted with the ejector-style exhausts, they still had the earlier radiator housing, and in any event, were actually coded DJ+KU, DP+KA, and TN+ZT. Ooops! However, if the standard spatted B-2 version is built, the skis could be saved to put on a model of a Ju 87D, of which several were so equipped in the field.

Ju 87D-5 (JT53 and 09053), Ju 87D-3N (07323) and Ju 87D-8 (09279)

First released around 1998, this Ju 87 D-5 kit shares the main fuselage and various other parts with the earlier Ju 87B kits, but has new long-span wings, new nose cowling parts, new canopy parts and the later type's refined undercarriage legs and spats.

The cockpit interior is a bit of a compromise though, featuring many common parts including the side walls and radios of the 'B', plus a new headrest/roll-over frame and MG 81Z rear-firing machine guns, but the instrument panel which was different on the 'D' is the same as the earlier 'B' kits' and for some reason, the rudder pedals that were included in the 'B' kits are missing in the 'D' boxings!

The surface detail is smooth with delicately engraved panel lines, and the new 'streamlined' engine cowling captures well the shape of the original. The assembly instructions are clear and simple to follow, breaking construction down into fifteen stages with additional diagrams highlighting where parts need modifying or holes drilled.

The new wings, again a full span lower half and two upper halves, feature simplified aileron and flap hinge mounts which are integrally moulded on the trailing edge of the lower wing half. Although this simplifies construction and provides a strong structure, it doesn't look as realistic as the Italeri and the new Airfix kits. The longer span wings were obviously modified from the original 'standard span' mouldings and leave a noticeable step where the longer wing tip, and extended aileron, were added and requires sanding.

The same bomb load as the 'B' is included, namely an SC 250 bomb and four SC 50s, for which there are two multi-purpose ETC 50/VIII fairings. Decals vary among the various boxings but include examples from StG 2, SG 5 and NSGr 2.

Ju 87G-2 (07360 and 09054)

This kit, released in 1998, was essentially the 'D' toolings (see above) with new parts added in the form of a pair of BK 37, 37mm anti-tank cannon each made up of two halves – one of which is moulded with the gun barrel, plus separate six-round magazines to be added to each side of the rear pod. The front and rear mounting supports are fitted to the top of each weapon. The cannon and their wing mounts are accurate in outline, although the cannon barrel muzzles are moulded solid and would benefit from being drilled out.

The decal sheet provides markings for two of Hans Ulrich Rudel's *Schlachtgeschwader* 2 aircraft with his *Kommodore*'s chevron and bars – one of which has the tactical yellow 'V' marking under the port wing introduced on aircraft operating over the Hungarian sector at the end of the war.

MONOGRAM 1/48 scale

Ju 87G-1 (PA207, 6840 and 74011)

This kit originally dates to 1968, and is typical of Monogram's older kits from this period – well moulded (in this instance in a dark green), with raised panel lines and featuring minimal cockpit interior detail comprising five pieces with raised details on the insides of the fuselage halves and two emaciated crewmen. Subsequently re-released at various intervals in 1970, 1973 and 1992, despite being marketed as a G-1, it was in fact a long wingspan G-2, and like the Hasegawa Stuka kits, had the aileron/flaps integrally moulded on the full-span one-piece lower wing trailing edge.

The four-part canopy was clear, and the pilot's hood and the gunner's section could be posed 'open' or 'closed'. The BK 37 cannon, moulded in halves with the barrel moulded in one of them, were basic but had separate magazine trays that fitted to integrally moulded racks under the lower wing half. Mainwheels were separate from the undercarriage spats and were surprisingly well, if a little inaccurately, detailed. The decal sheet had one option – markings for Rudel's T6+AD, which were commendably thin for the period and in register, with many of the stencils provided.

The kit was also released by Revell USA as a Ju 87D (5250). Although still based on the classic Monogram G-2 version's parts. Instead of the underwing BK 37 cannon pods, a centreline 500kg bomb and crutch, plus underwing bomb racks, four 50kg bombs and dive brakes were included, as were flame dampers for the exhausts and 20mm gun barrels for the wings. The flame dampers were moulded as a single piece with the interior side hollowed out and were designed to fit over the integrally moulded exhaust manifolds.

Decal options included Rudel's T6+AD, and in subsequent boxings, T6+BM of StG 2, Russia, 1943, and S2+KK, of 2./StG 77, Krim, 1943.

SPECIAL HOBBY 1/48 scale

Ju 87A (SH48007)

There was a vacform Ju 87A kit released in the 1980s, but other than that, Special Hobby (a part of the MPM empire), are the only manufacturer to have produced an injection-moulded kit of the 'Anton' in 1/48 scale.

The kit comes on two sprues of flash-free light grey plastic, with parts that have delicately engraved detail. The surface is very smooth, maybe too smooth, as the Stuka was not flush-riveted and was covered with a mass of rivet heads. The fuselage comes in full-length halves including the cowling and fin and rudder, with the cockpit interior made up of resin parts complete with a single, well-moulded, vacform canopy. The mainplanes are in five parts – an underside centre section with wing panels that include the undercarriage locations, two outer underwing sections and two upperwing halves. The ailerons and both sets of flaps are separate.

Decals are provided for 29•2, one of the three Ju 87A-1s used in the Spanish Civil War and for a Ju 87A-2 used on the eastern front for Stuka training and anti-partisan operations in 1943-44, coded TY+NJ.

REVELL 1/48 scale

Ju 87B-2
(Reboxing of Hasegawa kit)

TAMIYA 1/48 scale

Ju 87B-2 w/Bomb Loading Set (37008)
(Re-boxing of Italeri moulds)

HASEGAWA 1/32 scale

Ju 87G *Kanonenvogel* (08075 / ST25)
Originally released as a new tool in 2005, Hasegawa's Ju 87G comes in a large box with over 200 parts in grey plastic (forty-one of which are marked 'not for use' for this version). Eight parts are in clear plastic with five in white metal. The initial release also included a white metal figure of Hans Ulrich Rudel and an Alsatian dog.

Overall, general detail is good, there are no sink or ejector pin marks in visible areas and the kit has excellent surface detail with restrained but crisply engraved panel lines and rows of subtle rivets on all external metal-skinned surfaces.

The cockpit interior could maybe do with a little additional help, specifically with the radios, the twin 7.92 Zwilling machine guns (especially the gunsights) and the sidewalls. A pilot and a gunner figure are included. Fuselage assembly is straightforward but holes need to be pre-drilled for the add-on armour if it is to be fitted. The engine cowling and engine are separate sections and the fit is excellent.

The canopy is moulded in four parts, each commendably thin and free of distortion albeit a little brittle, so care needs to be taken when attaching them. The instructions don't depict an option to display them open, but in view of the relative thinness of the canopy hood it might be possible to sit the canopy over the top of central glazing. Frame lines are mostly marked on the inside, which is quite correct for the Stuka. Hasegawa also supplies decals to be applied to the inside of the canopy – another nice touch.

The wings comprise of a centre section consisting of upper and lower halves with an internal support spar. The outer wing sections are then added, the fit is good and ensures the correct dihedral is maintained. Like most Hasegawa kits, various parts are included which are planned for other variants, this one can be built as either a G-1 or G-2 and as such has separate standard, or long, outer wing tip panels that can be fitted. The mainwheels are produced in such a way, that they don't have to be trapped in the spats before painting, and can be added later.

The ailerons and flaps are supplied separately, as are the actuators. The latter are delicate and care needs to be exercised not to knock them off – especially during construction. The tailwheel assembly is nicely detailed in five parts, including a separate tie-down hook.

The 37mm cannon pods are adequate straight from the box, and Hasegawa has thoughtfully moulded the muzzle brake in two parts so the end is hollow, but the prominent cooling holes are simply represented as recessed circles. Bombs, wing racks and dive brakes are included (marked 'not for use'). Markings are supplied for two aircraft: Rudel's chevron and bar markings, and an aircraft coded GS+MD.

Ju 87D-1/D-5 (ST26)
The modelling fraternity didn't have long to wait for the second in the series to arrive, this time in the form of the Ju 87D-1/D-5. Again, the mouldings are first class, with no flash and are blemish free. The new additions to reflect the sub-type are in the form of two 300-litre underwing fuel tanks and attachment points, and a 1,000kg centreline bomb and crutch. All the other details are applicable from the G-1/G-2 kit boxing.

The twelve-page instructions are clear and precise and include two pages of colour scheme and decal plans, plus a page of paper masks for the splinter camouflage pattern. Surprisingly, the one thing Hasegawa have never added to their large-scale kits are seat belts. However, Eduard produce pre-painted seat belt sets for 1/32 scale Ju 87s which are worth investing in as they do add to the look of a finished cockpit if crew figures are to be excluded. The clear canopy parts are commendably thin, if a little brittle.

The decals cover two versions: a D-1/Trop of StG 3 coded S7+AA operating in Egypt in 1942, and Hans-Ulrich Rudel's D-5, T6+AD, Russia, summer 1944. The decals are well printed and in good register and include a full set of stencils for one aircraft, two styles of national marking (including swastikas) and the relevant individual aircraft marking.

REVELL 1/32 scale

Ju 87B (H-298, 4798)

Dating to the late 1960s, this kit, as expected, shows its age which, besides the raised panel line detail and a plethora of rivets covering all the external surfaces, includes the cockpit detail which is a little oversimplified, as are the mainwheel tyres. The spats are a dubious shape, and the exhaust manifolds and bombs are basic. Aircrew figures are included, but look like shop-window dummies. The kit has been re-released and re-boxed several times, and may have started life with markings for T6+MP of 6./StG with the snake design down the fuselage, and in a later boxing as S2+EK of 2./StG 77 with a yellow nose and rudder.

No longer generally available, it can still be found on the likes of eBay, although it has been superseded by the 2012 Trumpeter offering (also the 2008 '21st Century Toys kit' – see later – both of which have their own design and shape problems). However, with a bit of sanding and engraving of panel lines and perhaps some cross-kitting with the Trumpeter and 21st Century kits, as well as some aftermarket accessories, a more than acceptable model can still be achieved.

REVELL (GERMANY)

Ju 87D-1/G-1 (04711)

This Ju 87D-1/G-1, is thought to be a re-boxing of the Hasegawa kit. The kit's decal sheet features markings for three aircraft that served on the Eastern Front.

21st CENTURY TOYS 1/32 scale

Ju 87B/R

A new plastic construction kit company, 21st Century Toy's, appeared fleetingly in early 2008 with a range of 1/32 scale kits. Amongst the range was a Ju 87B/R and the kit became available in the UK via various modelling outlets, and then during the early summer of 2009 they ceased trading! At the time of writing no-one appears to have bought the moulds to resurrect this range of kits. The following notes are supplied by Tony Gloster who made this kit when it was first released.

21st Century Toy's kits came in a stout box containing nine plastic bags with around 109 well-moulded parts with no flash; and engraved, if somewhat heavy, panel lines like a Matchbox kit of old. The cockpit comprised twelve parts, but is basic with several injector pin marks on the cockpit sidewalls and floor.

The pilot's seat is the right shape but in need of thinning down around the sides and back, but the armour back plate is crudely moulded with injector pin marks just were it is hard to get to them.

A test fit of the cockpit tub revealed the need to remove the mounting points for the original instrument panel for which there is no instrument panel shroud. The pilot's underside observation window needs care in fitting. The other transparencies are clear, if somewhat thick, with the framing being very heavy. The first three canopy sections are just about okay, but the rear section is poor – completely the wrong shape in fact. The windscreen and centre sections come with huge mounting lugs and the fuselage halves and wing halves are held together with screws, (two for each wing and three for the fuselage). The screw holes are then covered with shaped plastic plugs to blend into the surfaces.

The two wing-mounted machine guns are not very good, but if you have a Hasegawa Stuka to hand, which has three types of gun covers, they fit the 21st Century kit's wing quite well! There are no mass balances for the ailerons, nor foot steps nor underside aerial mast!

The spinner is too narrow at its base and the undercarriage fairings will benefit from re-profiling the bottoms of the spats, but otherwise the fit to the wings is good and solid. The mainwheels are one-piece single items. The aileron/flap actuator rods are moulded in with the ailerons/flaps and have rather large lumps of plastic as mounting points on to the underside of the wings,

The instructions are in the form of eight A4 fold-out pages, which include a history, the eight section build, and the painting and decal placements for the three versions given: 6G+AT from 9./StG 51 France 1940; S2+LN of 5./StG 77 Austria 1941; and T6+BP of 6./StG, Libya 1941 – with the snake along its sides. The decals are very good indeed; you get a full set of stencils for one aircraft, a complete set of national marking and the relevant individual aircraft markings.

21st Century Toys were certainly not out to rival the likes of Hasegawa, but what they did is give the modeller a basic, reasonable accurate, example (apart from the poor canopy) of a Ju 87B, with a really excellent decal sheet.

TRUMPETER 1/32 scale

Ju 87A (03213)

Although the kit has certain shape and detail concerns it is unique, being the only Anton in this scale. The fit and parts assembly is good.

Ju 87B/R (03216)

Typical of Trumpeter, the kit is packed in to a sturdy box, containing some 330 well-moulded parts, which feature restrained engraved surface panel lines and subtle rivet detail. A complete engine is included, with optional open and closed radiator flaps. The detailed cockpit interior features an instrument panel with raised details, and includes decals to represent the instruments. There is a photo-etch set that includes additional cockpit bits like belts, levers, handles and such like. The front radiator grille is also in photo-etch as are straps for the 300-litre fuel tanks and some detail bits for the guns.

Although the main fuselage looks accurate enough, the nose section is apparently 2mm short and is noticeably narrow. This could be the reason the propeller spinner also appears smaller than it should be. The VS 5 propeller blades also seem a bit short which makes them look a bit broader than they should be.

The canopy of the Ju 87 had both internal and external framing, but like most of the other kit manufacturers, Trumpeter have moulded all the framing as external, so in this scale some creative painting will be needed to make this area look more accurate. There is an 'extra' rear canopy section included, however, per the instructions it is not to be used.

The fuselage has a pair of spars to slot into the wing roots to ensure the proper angle of the inverted gull wing as well as providing additional strength. The ailerons, flaps, rudder and elevators are all separate. The ailerons and flaps have moulded-on tabs where they attach to the wing, but the way the kit is designed, they are fixed in the neutral position. The dive brakes however are designed to be attached in the deployed position, which is a bit odd as they are normally

in the stowed 'up' position when the aircraft is on the ground. The wing gun bays are provided with photo-etch detail parts.

The wheel spats are the wrong shape. The lower-front part of the spat lacks the correct 'bulbous' curve effect, and the bottom of the spat has an incorrect more-or-less straight curve up from the front to the rear. Stubs are included for the undercarriage leg-mounted 'Jericho' sirens, but the propellers for these are not included. Rubberised vinyl tyres are provided for each wheel.

A variety of offensive weaponry is provided, including a bomb for the central underfuselage which looks to be nearer 1,000kg than the more standard 500kg or 250kg load. Four options exist for the outer wings – twin racks for either four 50kg bombs (although only two of the nominal four are included), a pair of 300-litre fuel tanks, (for a Ju 87R version), alternative racks each holding five smaller (5kg?) bombs, and finally, what looks to be a gun pod of some sort.

The kit comes with markings for three different aircraft – the aircraft featured on the box art, from 2./StG 2, Russian Front, late 1941 for which the unit's 'Scottie Dog' badge should face forward on both sides, but the decals are both facing the same way rather than being handed. The second aircraft is from 10./LG 1, based at Tramecourt, France, July 1940, and the third option is a winter camouflaged machine from *Stab* II./StG 1, Russian Front, December 1941. There is a multi-part swastika decal and some basic stencils included, but the upper wing crosses have strange proportions to them, with too much space in-between the white arms.

Instructions are in the usual landscape booklet format and provide colour information in a variety of paint brands. Arguably, while not perfect, this kit offers an improvement over the other two 1/32 scale 'Berta' options available today.

Ju 87D (3217)

Like several other manufacturers, Trumpeter have modified and/or utilised the original Ju 87B/R moulds to produce kits of the later D and G variants. Again comprising over 300 parts in light grey plastic, plus two clear sprues wrapped in thin foam on fourteen sprues, the revised dimensions and shapes look generally accurate.

The fuselage is moulded without the nose cowling sections, and there is a newly-tooled sprue for the more streamlined cowling of the D and G variants, moulded in two halves. A 30-part Jumo 211 engine is again included,

although there is no provision for displaying the engine, unless you leave off the forward cowling halves. Although these cowling halves are well detailed, they are moulded in vertically split halves, when they would have been better moulded in separate upper and lower sections, as on the real aircraft.

Interior fuselage detail is supplied on separate internal sidewalls. Detail is good with further cockpit detail including instrumentation panels, cockpit floor, seats, radios, control column, separate head armour. The upper section of forward fuselage, above the instrument panel area, and the dorsal fuselage section immediately aft of the rear gunner, are moulded separately.

The kit is designed so that the lower wing section incorporates both the inboard panels and the lower central fuselage, including the section for the bomb launch mechanism, the window and location points for the underwing radiators, for which, unfortunately, the cooling flaps can't be posed 'open' without surgery. There is a separate rudder and the tailplanes have separate elevators, although the elevator mass-balance has been moulded integrally with the forward curved section that is fitted to the tailplane tip and is set to 'neutral', which will involve some surgery if you want to display elevators 'offset'.

The main, outer wing panels are connected to the inboard sections by two spars that not only create extra rigidity, but also ensure the correct 'gull wing' angle is attained. Both the standard and long wingtips are provided, ostensibly allowing a D-1/D-3 or D-5/D-8 to be built, although only decals for Rudel's D-5, T6+AD, are included.

External wing and fuselage detail is good, with engraved panel lines, and rivet and fastener detail. Both gun bays are also well detailed so they can display the armament within, with rib detail, separate sidewall parts, MG17 gun breeches, breech plates, ammunition feeds and stub barrels. The wingtips are separate parts, and include the 'standard' and 'long-span' options.

The problems with the shape of the undercarriage spats on the Trumpeter Ju 87B kit, seem to have been resolved with those for the D/G variants, which seem okay, even though there is no provision for displaying the legs without the spats. But as the oleo legs themselves are reasonable, if you're willing to take out a saw and do a little surgery, then you could indeed display the struts. You might need to check the mainwheel hubs though, as they seem a little simple. Again, tyres are black vinyl.

The clear sprue parts, which are crystal clear, have good framing definition that will make masking an easier task, offers a number of options such as two different parts for the windscreen and pilot's sliding hood, one of which has separate side windows that can be posed either open or closed, and two variations for the gunner's hood, (although only one is shown in the instructions)

The propeller blades seem a little flat in section, but the shape looks reasonable. Various underwing bomb loads are supplied, including a centreline 500kg bomb, four 50kg bombs with optional percussion rods, two 66-litre fuel tanks, all with associated ETC racks, plus an unidentified machine-gun pod. The larger bomb has separate fins.

Ju 87G-2 (3218)

Not surprisingly, this kit is based upon the Ju 87D's mouldings and therefore offers essentially the same parts, with the same good surface detail and general accuracy.

'Standard' and 'long-span' wingtips and ailerons are included, for which the standard tips should be used for a G-1 and the longer versions for the G-2. The wings still have the options for the wing guns and associated armament bays – which are not applicable for the G-2 version for which a pair of 37mm cannon are included on an additional sprue. Although the underwing 37mm cannon barrels and pod fairings are well detailed, regrettably they are moulded handed when they were in fact symmetrically identical. The barrels are slide

moulded, meaning the muzzles are hollow.

Photo-etch parts include the ammunition feeds for the 37mm cannon, pilot's rear mirror, internal canopy handles, gunner's MG reticule parts and fuel tank straps, although no seat belts are included. Camouflage schemes and decal options for two Ju 87G-2s are provided – W.Nr 484110, and W.Nr 494193, both flown by Hans Ulrich Rudel of *Stab* SG in late 1944/early 1945.

AIRFIX 1/24 scale

Ju 87B-2 (18002)

The Ju 87 was a relatively large aeroplane, a fact certainly reflected by the very sizeable model it makes in 1/24 scale. Initially released in 1975 to much acclaim, it has subsequently been re-released with various new box top designs and decals, in 1996, 2005 and 2011. The kit was also re-boxed and released by MPC in 1982, with a change of decals

There are over 340 parts, moulded in a light grey plastic, which include a Jumo 211A-1 engine, and a sprue of clear parts. The mainwheels and tailwheel are moulded in black vinyl. All the surface detail panel lines are engraved and the rivets are a mixture of both recessed and raised.

The cockpit interior is good, if a little heavy in places, but will look fine once assembled and painted. The pilot's instrument panel comes in two parts, with a clear insert, featuring the dials which then fits into an instrument panel with holes moulded where the dials are meant to be, and again with careful painting will look fine. The pilot's seat could maybe do with thinning down a bit and reshaping a little to a more accurate profile, whereas the gunner's seat is fine, just requiring a careful clean-up and assembly. Two crew figures are included, with separate positionable heads, separate torsos, arms and legs, but there is no provision for seat belts. The transparent parts are clear and thin and the canopy features internal as well as external framing so careful masking is required.

The Jumo engine is well represented, with the engine bearers as part of the fuselage moulding allowing for a strong construction, and the kit has removable engine panels, although the air filter detail is a bit basic.

The wings are moulded in four parts and are joined along the break-line where the Stuka's distinctive inverted gull wing starts. The fit here is not too good and the join is weak, so internal reinforcement is worth considering. The outer sections contain the machine gun bays, with removeable panels, and the ailerons and flaps are separate. These control surfaces fit well and look good, although the underwing dive brakes are a little thick and could do with thinning down, as could the mainplane trailing edges.

The main undercarriage units can be modelled in either the 'landed' (laden) or 'flying' (unladen) mode. External ordnance is restricted to one 500kg centreline-mounted bomb and four wing-mounted 50kg bombs.

Decal choices have varied over the years, mainly including B-2s from StG 1 and StG 2 – the most recent box-top release featuring a pair of StG 2 machines, T6+MM of 4 *Staffel* in light tan areas painted over the original 70/71/65 as a temporary desert scheme and T6+KN of 6 *Staffel* in the standard 70/71/65 scheme.

Top: Eduard's Ju 87B/R combined with the Retrokit conversion to create the Ju 87C and their cockpit interior set. Complete replacement wings are provided for the carrier version along with the arrester hook. The various intakes and scoops were opened up and deepened where necessary. As the aircraft was trialled as a torpedo carrier I decided to fit an LTC carrier from the spares box in place of the bomb trapeze.

Above: The almost completed modelwith one wing fitted. The markings are partially conjectural so that I could add some colour. I also made the torpedo (I await a more detailed replacement) a 'training' round, hence the prominent red/white stripes. Note also the kit-supplied etched machine gun and tailplane struts. The kit also accurately captures the asymmetric intake on the nose – a feature missed by many.

Centre: These four views show added details including a pitot tube on the port wing and clear landing light cover on the starboard.

Below: On a suitable base, with its wings folded, the Ju 87C variant looks very different from other Stukas. *Model and photos by Mike Verier*

Top and centre left: The original 1950s 1/72 Airfix Ju 87B kit, (1395-91-01011) finished as S2+AM of 4./StG 77, serving in the Balkans in 1941 with yellow nose and rudder.

Centre right and bottom: The 1978/79 Airfix Ju 87B/R Series 2/ Series 3 range, (03030/ 01067) kit, finished as Ju 87B-2/Trop, T6+AM of 4./StG 2, Libya, May 1941, in a desert scheme produced by applying a sand colour, probably Italian *Giallo Mimetico* (Sand Yellow) over the original RLM 70/71 scheme.

Models and photos by Bill Newton

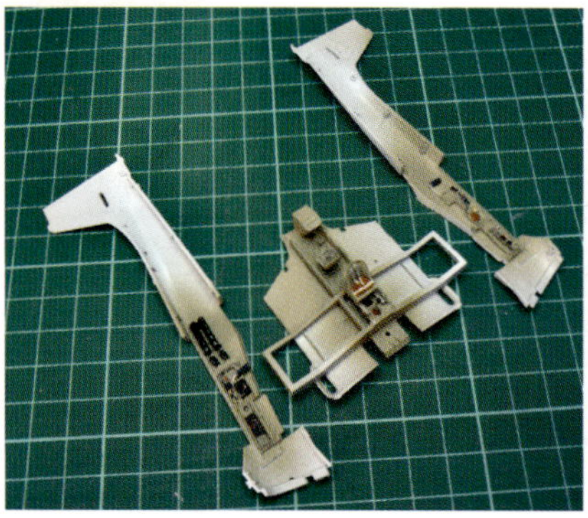

The 1/72 scale Airfix 2016 new-CAD design tool Ju 87B-1 kit (A03087) is moulded in a relatively soft light grey plastic, although the detail is sharp and very thorough. A small amount of flash was present on the smaller parts. A very substantial wing spar (part A18) was located onto the lower centre section and then all the cockpit details built onto this. The fit was very good.

This page and opposite page, top: The new Airfix 2016 model finished as Ju 87B-1, S2+EP of 6./StG 77 during the Battle of Britain.

The interior was airbrushed with RLM 02 and the detail then picked out with a fine brush. The instrument panel decal was used, which worked well and looked good.

The exhaust manifolds, (parts D08 and D09), were painted first and the cowling halves (parts D03 and D04) sprayed with RLM *Gelb*. Once the nose cowling had been assembled, the panel surrounding the exhaust stubs was masked, before the complete nose section was painted. This avoided the difficulty of cleanly painting around stubs. Part B09 needed some refining of the trailing edges.

It is best to paint all the sub-assemblies at this stage. For instance, the mainwheels need to be painted and masked before joining the undercarriage spat halves. The spinner cap, (part E04) in my kit was a short shot and had to be rebuilt.

AeroMaster RLM 70 and RLM 71 paints were used. The lower surfaces were painted with a mix to match RLM 65 *Hellblau*. The painting of the cockpit canopy (part E10) was difficult as some of the framing is seen through the slid-back pilot's canopy hood.

The dive brakes (parts B07 and B08) were not attached until after all the decaling had been completed; this allowed for the large underwing crosses to be placed into position. The small extra decals for the dive brakes can then be aligned after they have been added.

The model represents a Junkers 87B-1, S2+EP of 6./StG 77 during the Battle of Britain. The markings were from Xtradecal sheet X72249 while all the small stencilling decals were from the kit.

Below: Comparison views of the original 1950s Airfix Stuka and the latest 2016 release. *Models and photos by Bill Newton*

Airfix Ju 87B-2/R-2
Originally released in 1981 (05100-4), the kit was re-released with various box top illustrations in 1983 (9 05100), 1991 (05100) and in 2010 (A05100). It was also released by Heller in 1992, as part of the Airfix/Heller trading deal, with additional parts such as etch brass detail set and white metal exposed undercarriage legs.

This page: Ju 87B-2, T6+KL of 3./StG 2, St Malo, France, August 1940. *Model by Trevor Snowden: Photos by Bill Newton*

Opposite: Ju 87R-1, *werknummer* 5473, coded T6+CL of 3./StG 2, based in northern France, mid-July 1940. Typical of the dozens of Ju 87s used by the *Stukagruppen* during the opening stages of the Battle of Britain, this particular aircraft had upgraded ejector exhaust manifolds, and being the long-range version, was fitted with 300 litre drop tanks under the outer wings. *Model by Neil Robinson: Photos by Bill Newton*

Opposite page and above: Ju 87B-1, *werknummer* 2174, S2+AC of *Stab* II./StG 77, based in northern France, July/August 1940. A large proportion of the Ju 87s that operated against the British Isles were the original B variant, the B-1, with exhaust stubs rather than ejector manifolds and a fixed, rather than moveable, radiator flap. This particular model was made from the original Airfix Ju 87B/R boxing with an aftermarket replacement resin nose. *Model by Neil Robinson: Photos by Bill Newton*

Centre and bottom: Ju 87B-2/Trop, S7+KH of 1./StG 3, Cyrenaica, Libya, February 1941, finished in the factory-applied overall RLM 79 *Sandgelb* upper surfaces with RLM 80 *Olivgrün* mottle. *Model by Trevor Snowden: Photos by Bill Newton*

The brand new CAD-designed 1/48 scale Airfix Ju 87B-1 kit (A07114), released in January 2017 and finished as T6+GM, of 4./StG 2 in the spring of 1940. *Model and Photos by Rick Greenwood*

T6
GM

Hasegawa 1/48 Junkers Ju 87D-5 finished as an aircraft from 102/2 Dive Bomber Squadron, Hungarian Air Force, based at Kiniowo Airfield, Poland, June 1944.

Hasegawa's D-5 comprises 104 parts, (17 of which are not for use on the D-5), moulded in Hasegawa's usual grey plastic with eight clear parts. Generally, the moulding quality is very good except for the wingtips where there is a terrible mould-tool mismatch where they have added the extended tips. This area requires some filler, considerable sanding and re-scribing to restore the lost detail.

While Hasegawa has modified the wing tips to allow for the D/G sub-types, they did not change the wing root walkway areas from their earlier Ju 87B release. On early Stukas, the wingwalk areas were contained within three rectangular areas at the wing root, whereas the D/G Stukas had three areas with three raised ridges in each. After sanding away the existing wingwalk areas I used strips of plastic card with raised plastic card ridges glued on top.

The cockpit interior supplied by Hasegawa has some excellent detail, but also has a couple of glaring omissions – the rudder pedals (which I scratch built from Waldron photo-etched pedals mounted on plastic card supports), and the armoured headrest for the pilot, which I also made from plastic card.

The instrument panel was airbrushed RLM 66, and drybrushed with a lighter grey to pick out the details. Some of the smaller instrument bezels were finished in red and yellow followed by Mike Grant instrument decals added one at a time. When dry the decals were each given a drop of Klear/Future to create the impression of glass faces on the dials. The remainder of the cockpit was finished in RLM 66, given a dark wash and then various light grey dry brushings, with smaller details were picked out with black, red and yellow. Eduard photo-etched Luftwaffe seat belts were then added.

Some of the clear canopy parts need to have the framing painted on the inside – references need to be checked to see which frames are internal and which are external. I originally planned to use the kit's pilot's sliding canopy, but could not get it to sit properly over the fixed piece so ended up vacforming a replacement canopy.

One area where I feel Hasegawa compromised on accuracy, was the way they moulded the actuators for the control surfaces on the wings, as solid chunks of plastic, so I cut away all the linkages and replaced them with sections of brass wire – while not 100% accurate, they are far more realistic than those Hasegawa provided.

The painting steps for this model were a rather long and complicated process, partially because I had to carefully mask off and paint some of the markings as decals were not available. Xtracolor X202 RLM 65 *Hellblau* was sprayed on the undersurfaces, and using appropriately-sized masks I sprayed on Xtracolor X201 RLM 02 to represent overpainted underwing Luftwaffe crosses. The under surfaces were then masked off and the upper surfaces were airbrushed with Xtracolor X205 RLM 71 *Dunklegrün*. After it had thoroughly dried, I applied raised edge masks for the splinter pattern camouflage as, if you carefully study photographs of Stukas finished in RLM 70/71 it is noticeable that the demarcation between the two greens is not a true hard edge. I then applied X204 RLM 70 *Schwarzgrün* to complete the upper surface painting. Of note is the low contrast between the two greens – some brands of RLM 71 model paint are far too light with too much contrast resulting.

Xtracolor X201 RLM 02 was airbrushed over the area where the original fuselage codes and the swastika would have been on a Luftwaffe machine. Again, these were raised edge masks as I wanted a slightly softened demarcation to give the impression that the areas were originally sprayed 'free hand'. The national insignia, squadron crests and stencils were from AeroMaster decal sheet 48-140 'Stuka Bombers', and I made vinyl masks for the numeral '3' on the mainwheel spats and the 'B.7+ 03' on the fuselage. A medium grey wash was applied to all panel lines, followed by small amounts of silver paint to represent paint chipping and general areas of wear. Finally, chalk pastels were applied to create fading and signs of general usage. The aerial wire was made from stretched sprue and the insulators from drops of white PVA glue.

Model by Randy Lutz: Photos by Jamie Leggo

B.7

03

B.7
03

B.7
03

B.7
03
3

B.7
03

B.7
03
3

Airfix 1/24 scale Ju 87B-2/Trop, finished as T6+AM, 4./StG 2, Gambut, Libya, October 1941, finished in Italian *Giallo Mimetico* bands over the original RLM 70/71 'greens' scheme. *Model and photos by Bill Newton*

Airfix 1/24 scale Ju 87B-2, finished as J9+BL, of 3./StG 1, based at Angers, France, August 1940 – in the Airfix kit box scheme and decals. *Model by Trevor Snowden: Photos by Bill Newton*